Creole Meets English

by

JACQUES JULMICE

TOOT MOON LEE
Publishing

DEDICATION

This resource is dedicated to my late father, François Victorin, who would have been so proud that his son is an author and to my mother, Yvette, for her love and for molding me into the man that I am today. It's also dedicated to my beautiful wife, Nancy, for her support in all that I undertake and for her endless prayers for the entire family. My goal for writing is to help my native country, Haiti, to overcome and play a significant role in eradicating illiteracy in Haiti by the year 2030. I also want to inspire my kids, Nylah and Aneesa, and anyone who reads this book, especially the youngsters to share their knowledge and expertise through writing.

Author's Note

Many people unequivocally believe that learning a language is only for a chosen few. If you are one of those people or used to be one of those people, I invite you to have an open mind, explore the first few pages of this resource and allow me to show you how easy it is to learn Creole (Kreyòl). I'm not denying that some people have found it difficult and have had to put in a lot of effort before becoming fluent in a language while others have had an easier time of it. However, I've found the formula that makes the task easier for all and present it here in logical steps to enable you to become conversational with minimal effort and fluent with daily and consistent practice.

Kreglish is a new methodology that I developed that makes Creole accessible to anyone who speaks English and enables anyone to begin speaking the language within hours of using this book. In fact, you can begin speaking right from the back cover. I know you're probably thinking it's easy for me to say because it's my mother tongue. However, by using the Kreglish methodology during the beginning stages of your learning experience, you have the luxury of skipping the traditional hard stuff and jumping right into speaking. Allow me to teach you how to hack Kreyòl. You don't need to have an extensive vocabulary or know how to conjugate verbs to begin speaking. Based on my experience, pronunciation is arguably the most difficult aspect of a new language, but we'll use English pronunciation to get started. And I'll indicate what you need to focus on to transition what you already know in English into Kreyòl.

Dedication and passion make everything easier. Apply what you learn here, and practice hard and you'll surprise yourself! If you're passionate about learning Kreyòl, you'll be fluent in no time. I've worked with learners who've achieved fluency in a very short period of time. Just like many English speakers, their confidence wasn't the highest when they began, but once they got over the fear and doubt and discovered that Kreglish makes learning Kreyòl easy and fun, their experience became pleasant; and the more they learned, the more passionate they became. Are you ready to have some fun with me? Let's do this!

How the Book is Organized

You'll begin speaking in the next few minutes using English words pronounced in English that sound Creole. Believe it or not, you already have a rich Creole vocabulary, but you weren't aware of it up to now. We reveal those words that you already know and teach you how to use them in sentences and conversations. Slowly but surely, we transition you to reading Creole. At some point, deep into the text, we completely omit some English words that we use repeatedly and replace them with Creole words you should be familiar with by then.

The Kreglish methodology offers an innovative alternative to learning Creole. Instead of using the traditional route of cramming vocabulary and spending an enormous amount of time on grammar and conjugation, we dive into conversation right away. Even if you're a complete newbie, you'll learn meaningful and practical sentences, which you're able to pronounce from day one. I've incorporated English words that sound Kreyòl and other words that are spelled the same in both languages in my teaching, and that has made a huge difference in my students' ability to become conversational in a short period of time. I have no doubt it will be the same for you as well.

Practice Makes Perfect

Every once in a while, you'll come across some practical conversations. Ideally you should work through them with a partner, but if you don't have access to one, practice both sides of the conversation or join our growing community at haiti2030.org to practice with someone who like you, may also need a partner with whom to practice.

About Me

Thank you for your support of this Creole-learning resource, which is designed to introduce you to the Creole language or enhance your understanding of it. If you're a native speaker and have never learned to write the language, if growing up, you never learned your mother tongue, if you're a missionary, relief worker, including medical professionals, who wants to better communicate with a Creole speaking community, if you're an adoptive parent, if you plan to travel to travel to a Kreyòl speaking country, or if your significant other's native tongue is Kreyòl, this book is for you.

My name is Jacques Julmice. I was born in Port-au-Prince, Haiti, but consider the city Dessalines, the namesake of the father of independence, my hometown. While my family spoke Kreyòl at home, the school I attended only taught in French, a remnant of colonization. Although Haiti was colonized by many European nations over the years, France had the biggest influence, as it had the longest stay on the small Caribbean island that was called the "Jewel of the Caribbean" during colonial times for its abundant natural resources and treasures.

I enjoyed learning foreign languages at a very young age. In high school, I wasn't satisfied with just submitting my English or Spanish homework and getting good grades on my exams, I took it one step further and practiced conversations out loud. Since my siblings and friends refused to practice with me and thought I was insane, I used to stand in front of a mirror or ride my roller skates back in the early 80's and practice both sides of passionate conversations. By the time I graduated high school, I was conversational in both Spanish and English. That was a tremendous advantage when I migrated to the Boston area in 1985 and attended Roxbury Community College for one semester to hone my listening skills. My knowledge of Spanish was also quite useful in that environment as the majority of the student body was from Central and South America and spoke Spanish. I became fluent in Spanish as well as I had the opportunity to practice nearly every day with classmates and friends.

After completing my undergraduate degree in Electronics Engineering at Wentworth Institute of Technology in Boston, Massachusetts, the US economy was struggling, and I had a hard time finding full-time employment as an engineer. The only job I could find was to work as an interpreter and translator for my compatriots who couldn't speak English. I went on to have a thirty-year career in high-tech that's still ongoing and earned my MBA along the way. Looking back, that translator job was arguably the most rewarding of my life. It was an honor to give a voice to my brothers and sisters who couldn't communicate in the language of the adopted country they called home.

I went on to learn to write in Kreyòl, a skill that very few native Creole speakers possess, some by choice choosing to favor French, while others, because of their social status, they unfortunately never had the opportunity to go to school and learn to read and write in any language. According to the latest statistics from renowned world organizations and non-governmental organizations, Haiti's population has been growing at a rate of 1.2 percent per year. The Haitian population reached 11.1 million by 2018, and the literacy rate was believed to be 60 percent. However, most Haitians I talk to feel this number is politicized and the real number is closer to 10 percent literacy.

I created a blog haiti2030.org to teach Haitians as well as foreign nationals to speak, read, and write Kreyòl so that I can give back and contribute to the development of my country. The blog led to extensive research, which was transformed to sheer passion, some novel discoveries, and my personally developed methodology of using English to teach Kreyòl. I call the methodology KREGLISH.

Before we embark on this journey, I want to share with you a couple of terms that I coined, which I invite you to get familiar with. The first one is R2R, which stands for Relate to Remember. The scientific term is *mnemonic*. However, when I started using this technique in the early 1980s, I wasn't sophisticated enough to know such a big word. It was only recently that I discovered that it's an actual thing, a memory aid, a scientifically proven technique. Here is how I suggest you use it: for most of the words and expressions that you're learning here with me, there's an opportunity to create some type of relationship in your mind to help you memorize what you learn. What you're learning is foreign to you, but if you can relate it to something in your environment that you're comfortable with, your odds of retention increase by a wide margin. The R2R technique has worked beautifully for me over the years, helping me become fluent in four languages: English, French, Spanish, and Creole. I've also learned a few words in at least twenty other languages using the R2R technique. It's an integral part of my teaching, and I'm confident it'll be an effective tool for you as well.

I also coined the term Killilliteracy, which is a combination of *kill* and *illiteracy*. My mission as an author is to eradicate illiteracy in Haiti, but it won't be possible without your support. I'm asking for the support of every one of my readers, not to donate money (there's too much of that going on), but to learn Kreyòl, to read this book and the ones I'll publish in the future, and to use them as tools to teach others. You'll realize right into the first few pages that learning Creole is very much within reach and realatively easy. Are you able to teach someone how to spell *al, ale, gate, pike,* or *pale*? If you answered in the affirmative, then you already have enough knowledge to begin teaching an illiterate Creole speaking kid to read and write. By the way, the above are also Kreyòl words. Over the next few pages you will learn how to pronounce them and others just like them in Kreyòl and to use R2R to memorize their meaning.

Kreglish, which is a combination of Kreyòl and English, is the whole premise of my methodology. Simply put,

1. It's the art of reading English words and sentences that sound Kreyòl, which help you master pronunciation right away. One example is the Kreyòl word **moun**, which sounds just like [*moon*], but means people. We also have our own version of [*full moon*] in terms of pronunciation only. In Kreyòl, it's spelled **foul moun**, which means a crowd. We take advantage of the common pronunciation and share some techniques to enable you to memorize the meanings of those words.

4

2. It's also the use of a large number of words that are spelled identically in both languages, to help improve your vocabulary. One caveat here is that the meanings of those words are completely different between the two languages. The advantage is that you can spell them. We'll work together on the meaning and pronunciation. For example, you can spell the word *"men"*, but it has nothing to do with a person; it has more than one meaning, but for now we'll stick with one of the most common meanings, which is **hand**.

3. It also incorporates the use of cognates that are words descended from the same language or form. The difference between this group and the last one is that the meaning is the same across the different languages. Those words have the same root across multiple languages; in most cases the spelling and pronunciation are different, but there are a few cases where the spelling is identical or very close to each other. One such example is the verb **to adore**, which is the exact same word **adore** in Kreyòl and **adorer** in French. We can even throw in Spanish: **adorar**, Portuguese: **adoro**, and Italian: **adorare**. You'll learn to recognize the cognates by using our substitution rules, which will exponentially improve your vocabulary.

Thank you for joining me on this journey of learning Kreyol.

Table of Contents

Part I

Introducing the
KREGLISH METHODOLOGY

Conversation

Below is a conversation between two individuals where the first enquires about the invitation she sent to Ashley & Abigail to come visit her, and the second shares each person's plan with respect to the invitation. The left column is made up of English words that are sequenced in such a way to make what you read sound like a Creole sentence. Where you see a capital letter by itself, read it as a standalone letter of the alphabet but do not pause between letters or words. There is no comma in any of the sentences; let it flow as if there's no pause. Read each row as if you're reading a sentence and if you have someone next to you or someone you can call on the phone who speaks Creole, read each sentence to them and have them translate to confirm that they understand what you say.

English that sounds Kreyòl	Translation
Coat Ashley?	Where's Ashley?
Lee pap Vinny	She isn't coming
Poo key?	Why?
Pass K lee Pat con seem tap Vinny	Because she didn't know I was coming
A P lee Pat D boss lee seal tap Vinny	And she didn't tell her boss she was coming
Lap Vinny lot Sam D	She's coming next Saturday
A T moon yo?	How about the kids?
T moon yo Pat Sue Vinny	The kids weren't up to it
A Abigail?	How about Abigail?
Lap Vinny	She's coming
Key lot moon cap Vinny?	Who else is coming?
Lot moon yo pap Vinny	The other people aren't coming
Abigail app Vinny poo call	Abigail's coming alone
S K lee Sue woot?	Is she on the way?
We, lee D K lee Sue woot	Yes, she said that she's on the way
Map Vinny poo come too	I'm also coming alone

12

Congratulations! You just had a meaningful and relatively lengthy conversation in Creole; one that can potentially happen in real life, but you used English words exclusively. If you ever had any fear this was going to be challenging, I want you to throw any kind of worry out of the window and be confident that together, you and I will make this easy and fun. From the preceding conversation, you can capture more than 30 vocabulary words. Now is the perfect time to whip out your preferred note-taking instrument and begin noting some important vocabulary, expressions, and concepts. For example:

1. Coat means where.
2. Lee means she or he.
3. The letter A means how about.
4. D means to say or to tell.
5. K means this or that.
6. The letter S followed by K, like S K, is the combination that begins most questions.
7. Vinny means to come.
8. Boss is pronounced the same way as its Kreyòl equivalent and means the same; it's actually borrowed from English.
9. Lot means other.
10. Lap means he's / she's followed by a verb ending in ing.
11. Key means who or what.
12. Too pronounced in English has the same meaning in Creole: too = tou.
13. Moon means people.
14. The letter T followed by moon like T moon means kids.
15. Con means to know.
16. Pat means didn't.

There are of course many more words and expressions that you can note from the preceding conversation, but more importantly, right from the start, you're getting used to pronunciation. I hope you realize how easy this can come to you if you let it. You're technically reading English but when you put it all together, it sounds like you're speaking Creole (Kreyòl) and your pronunciation is close to perfect.

Note that the Kreyòl spelling of the words in the first column is different, but I want to focus on pronunciation at this point. I left out the Creole spelling to keep the table simple and avoid confusion. Later you'll see the correct Kreyòl spelling, which is quite different in most cases.

When you see examples similar to the above, you should put a special emphasis on pronunciation when taking notes. Keep in mind that since Creole is a phonetic language, the sound of each letter and blend is constant. For example, the translation of the word *"who"* is **ki**, which is pronounced *"key,"* and **i** always sounds like **ee**. That will never change; since Kreyòl is a phonetic language, the sound of each letter or blend is constant.

We haven't even gotten to the introduction and you've already had a conversation and sounded like a native speaker. There are some who spend years studying a foreign language and never learn as much as you have learned on day one. Maybe you're one of those who knew a bit of French, German or Spanish in high school and forgot it all. Not to worry, with Kreglish, the degree of difficulty doesn't increase; if anything, it becomes easier. I'd never want to hear you say, "I used to know a bit of Kreyòl, however ..." This method is meant for you to learn it and keep it forever!

Introduction

It may come as a surprise, but there are many similarities between English and Creole. Kreglish takes full advantage of these similarities and is so effective that you can begin speaking Creole today. Come to think of it, you just did, didn't you?

This resource makes no presumptions about your level. It's ideal for day-one beginners as it lets you begin your journey in familiar territory. It's also efficient for intermediate and advanced learners wishing to improve their vocabulary, pronunciation, and conversation. For native speakers who don't know how to write Kreyòl yet, you finally have everything you need in one place to correctly write your mother tongue.

Within, you are given the invaluable opportunity to build your Creole vocabulary using English words and simple pronunciation cues. Yes, that's correct—my methodology encourages you to take advantage of what you already know to enhance your Kreyòl learning experience. Kreyòl has more in common with English than has been taught in the past. In fact, when it comes to writing in Kreyòl, it is ironically closer to English than it is to French. This is difficult for some to understand, as Kreyòl is extremely close to French, but only in terms of pronunciation and inflection—reading and writing are much different.

Imagine learning a foreign language and before you even begin the journey you find out there are hundreds of words that you can already spell because their spelling is identical to some English words. There also are thousands more words, starting with the letters of the alphabet that sound similar to English words or phrases.

The following table contains another set of similarities called cognates that are words descended from the same language or form. Because of the French influence on both English and Kreyòl, the three languages sharef many cognates. In most cases the spelling is different, but with a little bit of practice, which you will gain in this resource, you will be able to easily recognize them even when they are spelled differently. The following talbe contains perfect cognates between Creole and English because the spelling is identical. However, the French version of the same word is slightly different.

French Vs. English / Kreyòl Spelling

Note that the Kreyòl spelling is identical to English

French	English	Kreyòl [pronunciation]
Aspirine	Aspirin	Aspirin [ahs-pee-reen]
Banque	Bank	Bank [bahNk]
Agoniser	Agonize	Agonize [ah-goh-nee-zey]
Bâton	Baton	Baton [bah-tohN]
Demande	Demand	Demand [da-mahNd]
Plante	Plant	Plant [plahNt]
Révoquer	To Revoke	Revoke [rey-voh-key]
Salade	Salad	Salad [sah-lahd]
Solide	Solid	Solid [soh-leed]
Soupe	Soup	Soup [soop]
Timide	Timid	Timid [tee-meed]
Vitamine	Vitamin	Vitamin [vee-tah-meen]

This book contains a collection of words that are either spelled the same or have very close spellings in both English and Creole. For example, some of my favorite words in terms of their closeness to English are the quartet: m*ens, women, woman,* and *womans*. Surely, this sounds weird to you—your first reaction upon seeing these words may be to question my knowledge of English, for how on earth could I put an *s* on the end of words like man and woman without an apostrophe? You probably think this is one of the first rules I should know about the English language. Indeed, that was among the first set of rules I learned in high school during my very first year of learning English as a second language. But the words I've shared are actually Kreyòl words with completely different meanings and pronunciation than you are used to:

> *Mens* [mehNs] translates to **"thin"** as in a thin person
> **Woman** [woh-mahN] translates to "**romantic novel**"
> *Womans* [woh-mahNs] translates to "**romance**"
> *Women* [woh-mehN] translates to "**Roman**"

In the early chapters, I share with you some tips and tricks to take advantage of said similarities. In the later chapters, I cover the Creole alphabet and introduce the words with the same or similar spelling. Besides the cognates that are words descended from the same language or form, most of the similarities, are purely coincidental. Neither the influence of France on England, nor the borrowing of English words from the American occupation of 1915 to 1934 under President Woodrow Wilson, following the assassination of then President Vilbrun Guillaume Sam, constitute a great number of said similarities. The similarities are, in fact, due to one key characteristic of Kreyòl: while English borrowed many words from French, the spellings of those words are quite different between the two languages. However, because Kreyòl is a phonetic language, it does not inherit from French the complex spelling of certain words featuring multiple silent letters. With few exceptions, a phonetic language is characterized by letters that are pronounced 100 percent of the time. There is a one-to-one relationship in which every letter makes a unique sound and every sound is represented by a unique letter or blend. Because of that simplicity, Kreyòl is in fact closer to English in many aspects and that is what my teaching is based on.

My ultimate goal is to get you started using Kreyòl words that you already know from English, which in my opinion, are much easier to remember. You can begin formulating sentences using those words to get ahead of the game. I do not believe in cramming vocabulary words; taking advantage of words you already know is much more effective. You know how to read and write these words—I'll just help you appropriate their pronunciation and meaning to the Kreyòl environment.

Various research findings suggest a strong correlation between the number of vocabulary words known in a certain language and overall proficiency in speaking that language. One such finding states that you only need five hundred common vocabulary words to be able to engage in basic conversation and four thousand to be considered an advanced speaker. Using my method, you can achieve both levels of proficiency midway through this book.

As you work through this resource, you will use your command of English vocabulary and concepts to easily transition to Kreyòl, using the following approach:

1- Practice pronunciation using letters of the English alphabet that sound just like Kreyòl words.
2- Take advantage of Kreyòl words or expressions that sound like English to learn pronunciation.

3- Improve pronunciation right away. While pronouncing English words arranged in a sequence to sound like Kreyòl sentences, you'll learn to pay attention to the sounds of the vowels, which account for close to 90 percent of what you need to pronounce Kreyòl correctly. For the most part, the sound of the consonants do not differ much between both languages.

4- Familiarize yourself with words that are spelled identically in English and Kreyòl, like *ale, ban, gate,* **and** *pale*. By applying pronunciation tips from step 1, you will also be able to pronounce these words.

5- Using my R2R, or "Relate to Remember," technique you'll be able to easily retain what you learn.

6- Quickly build a base vocabulary using the large number of short one, two, or three letter words that are relatively easy to remember.

7- Enhance your ability to retain and recall vocabulary by using English nicknames like Dan, Fran, Kay, Kim, Jodi, Mo, Pam, and Zak, which are spelled like Kreyòl words.

8- Continue to enhance your vocabulary by recognizing common English acronyms like AP and PA and two-letter state abbreviations, thirteen of which, like RI and LA, are actual Kreyòl words.

THE BASICS

1. Letters of the English Alphabet That Sound like Kreyòl Words.

There are ten English letters that sound exactly like Kreyòl words: *a, b, c, d, k, o, p, s, t,* and *v.* To avoid confusion, only eight out of ten are included in the chart below. To understand how to use the chart, let's analyze the smaller rectangle on the left. The letter *c* pronounced in English sounds like the Kreyòl word uner it: *si*, which means "*if*" as seen in the bigger rectangle on the right.

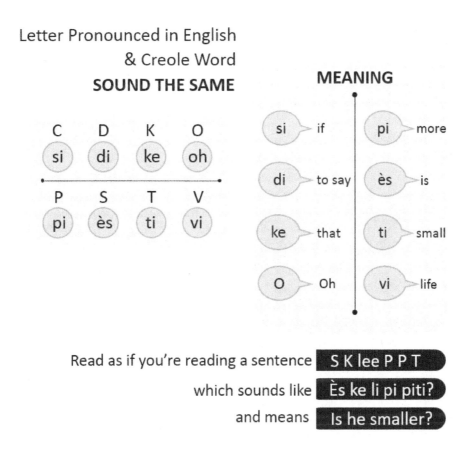

Read as if you're reading a sentence   **S K lee P P T**

which sounds like   **Ès ke li pi piti?**

and means   **Is he smaller?**

These words can be combined to create a large variety of sentences that absolute beginners can read right away. Choose a few to incorporate in your vocabulary on day one and add a few more each day. My suggestion is to start with *k, c, d, p,* and *s*, which you'll encounter in a variety of sentences.

The advantage of starting your learning process with these words is that it affords you the ability to practice and master pronunciation early on, granting you a tremendous advantage. Based on my experience, pronunciation is the most difficult aspect of learning a new language. However, since you're starting out using English letters and words that you already know how to pronounce, the whole experience becomes less challenging. You can gain close to perfect pronunciation right away.

2. Letter Combinations Pronounced in English that Sound Kreyòl

We can continue to use the English alphabet to learn Creole by combining letters pronounced in English in groups of two or three. These combinations are made up of the letters we saw earlier. The examples below translate to common words like *then, spicy, smaller, and cap and the* second and third column sound the same for easy pronunciation.

English	Pronounced in English	Kreyòl
cap	K P	kepi
is it	S K	ès ke
pee	P P	pipi
then	A P	epi
small	P T	piti
small	T P T	ti piti
small cap	T K P	ti kepi
small amount of pee	T P P	ti pipi
smaller, smallest	P P T	pi piti
spicy, to poke, to dive	P K	pike
so small	2 P T	tou piti
so spicy	2 P K	tou pike
what if	A C	e si

Given Kreyòl's closeness to English we have the advantage of composing sentences right off the bat by combining letters of the English alphabet with familiar words pronounced in English. The way the letters are sequenced means nothing in English, but when pronounced in English, they end up being perfect Kreyòl sentences.

Here's how to use the examples in the table that follows: Read the big bold letters and words on the right side of the table as if you're reading a sentence. What you read sounds just like the Kreyòl sentence in the bold font at the bottom left. The meaning of what you said in Kreyòl is in the lighter font above the Kreyòl sentence.

Meaning **Kreyòl spelling** (same pronunciation as cell to the right)	Read in English
Are they small? **Ès ke yo piti?**	S-K yo P T?
They said that they are smaller **Yo di ke yo pi piti**	Yo D K yo P P T
Are their lives hard? **Ès ke vi yo di?**	S K V Yo D
They said that life is hard **Yo di ke vi a di**	Yo D K V ah D

Using the above technique, we can produce hundreds or even thousands of sentences. In order to build your vocabulary at your own pace, choose the words and expressions you find most useful to memorize before continuing.

You can easily begin the majority of Kreyòl questions using three of the four combinations below, all of which can be pronounced using words or letters pronounced in English?

- *Ès ke,* sounds like *S K*, and means "**is it**"
- *Ki ès*, sounds like *key S,* and means "**who is**"
- *Pou ki*, sounds like *poo key,* and means "**why**"
- *Paske*, sounds like *pass K, and* means "**because**"

You can use those expressions to immediately begin asking and answering questions:

Question

Poo key lee Pat fell

sounds like: *Pou ki li pa t fè L?*

and means: *Why didn't she do it?*

Answer

Pass K lee Pat con pool fell.

sounds like: *Paske li pa t konn pou L fè L.*

and means: *Because she didn't know she had to do it.*

Besides the letters, there are many English words that also sound Kreyòl. For example using the group of words below, we can make up more complex sentences that you can also pronounce easily.

English & Creole Phrases that

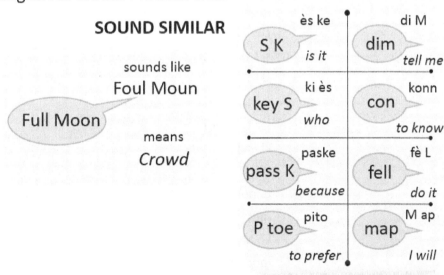

Read as if you're reading a sentence **Lee con key S key fell**

which sounds like **Li konn ki ès ki fè L**

and means **He knows who did it**

Below are some additional words and expressions that sound Kreyòl.

English	Kreyòl [sounds like]
a bunch	foul [full]
alone, by himself / herself	pou kò L [poo call]
alone, by myself	pou kò M [poo come]
also, too	tou [too]
as if	kòm si [come C]
crowd	foul moun [full moon]
didn't	pa t [Pat]
do it	fè L [fell]
every	chak [shaq]
for	pou [poo]
girl	fi [fee]
he or she must	fò L [fall]
his / her body	kò L [call]
his / hers	pou L [pool]
his / hers	pou li [pully]
hot	cho [show]
if he / she ...	si L [seal]
if I ...	si M [seem]
if they ...	si yo [C yo]
if we ...	sin N [seen]
who / what	ki [key]
little girl	ti fi [T fee]
little kids	ti moun [T moon]
must, owner, meter	mèt [met]
my body	kò M [come]
people	moun [moon]
see it	wè L [well]
table	tab [tab]
tell him / her	di L [dill]
tell me	di M [dim]
tell them	di yo [D yo]

tell us	di N [dean]
to come	vini [vinny]
to go out	soti [so T]
to know	konn [con]
we must	fò N [fawn]
who	ki moun [key moon]
who / what	ki [key]
why	pou ki [poo key]

While the previous sentences were mostly made up of the letters that sound Kreyòl, we can expand on the concept by formulating more complex sentences using some of the words in the preceding table.

Meaning **Kreyòl spelling** (same pronunciation as cell to the right)	**Read in English**
What did you say? **Ki sa W di?**	Key Saudi
Who said it? **Ki ès ki di L?**	Key S key dill
Who is the owner of the tables? **Ki ès ki mèt tab yo?**	Key S key met tab yo
She's the one who said it **li k di L**	Leak dill
She's going out too **L ap soti tou**	Lap so T too

They didn't know the plates were dirty **Yo pa t konn si plat yo sal**	Yo Pat con C plat yo Sal
They didn't say they knew the owners **Yo pa t di si yo konn mèt yo**	Yo pat D C yo con met yo
He told me who did it **Li di M ki ès ki fè L**	Lee dim key S key fell
They told me they know who did it **Yo di M yo konn ki ès ki fè L**	Yo dim yo con key S key fell
The plates are so hot **Plat yo tou cho**	Plat yo too show
The plates that are on the table are dirty **Plat ki sou tab yo sal**	Plat key sue tab yo sal
He or she must do it **Fò L fè L**	Fall fell
He said he must do it **Li di fò L fè L**	Lee D fall fell
He said we must do it **Li di fò N fè L**	Lee D fawn fell
They didn't know who asked that it be done **Yo pa t konn ki moun ki bay fè L**	Yo pat con key moon key by fell
She knows who's going to do it for her **Li konn ki ès L ap bay fè L**	Lee con key S lap by fell

She admits that the kids' lives are hard **Li admèt ke vi ti moun yo di**	Lee add met K V T moon yo D
It's such a small crowd **Foul moun yo tou piti**	Full moon yo too P T
He can come **Li mèt vini**	Lee met Vinny
He can go out **Li mèt soti**	Lee met so T
How about the kids? **E ti moun yo?**	A T moon yo
How about the little ones? **E sa k tou piti yo?**	A sack too P T yo
How about the smaller ones? **E sa k pi piti yo?**	A sack P P T yo
She told me she's coming next Saturday **Li di M ke L ap vini lòt samdi**	Lee dim K lap Vinny lot Sam D
It's longer than the others **Li pi long ke lòt yo**	Lee P long K lot yo
She said the kids aren't coming **Li di ti moun yo pap vini**	Lee D T moon yo pap Vinny
He said he knows who's coming **Li di L konn ki moun k ap vini**	Lee dill con key moon cap Vinny

Do they know why? **Ès ke yo konn pou ki?**	S ke yo con poo key
Do they know why she did it? **Ès ke yo konn pou ki L fè L?**	S ke yo con poo kill fell
Yes, they know why she did it **Wi, yo konn pou ki L fè L**	We yo con poo kill fell
Yes, they know who said it **Wi, yo konn ki ès ki di L**	We yo con key S key dill
Because he's wearing a mask **Paske li maske**	Pass K lee mass K

Question
S K lee dean poo key?
sounds like: Ès ke li di N pou ki?
and means: *Did he tell you all why?*

Answer
Lee D lee pat con poo key.
sounds like: Li di li pa t konn pou ki.
 and means: *He said he didn't know why.*

Kreyòl Pronunciation

Few discrepancies exist between English and Kreyòl pronunciation of consonants; most of the differences involve the vowels, nasals, and a few key blends. Once you master those, your ability to speak will naturally improve, but that might take a little while. I want you to instead focus on your ability to read Creole, which is technically possible once you're able to pronounce the following vowels and key blends.

- **A** is pronounced **ah**, but with a less drawn-out sound because the **h** is silent. This effectively shortens the vowel. Example: **a, ka, la, pa, sa, ta**.
- **E** is pronounced like **ey** like *"obey"* not *"key."* Again, you want to end the vowel sound earlier by excluding the **y** *sound.* Example: **e, de, ke, se, te**.
- **È** is pronounced like the short **e** in *"let, met,* and *net."* Example: **kè, lè, sè, wè, lèt, mèt, nèt, sèt, tèt, vèt**.
- **I** is pronounced **ee**; end the sound briskly. Example: **ki, li, ni, si, ti, vi, wi**.
- **O** is pronounced **oh**; end the sound briskly; don't pronounce the **h** at the end. Example: **do, fo, lo, mo, po, poko**.
- **Ò** sounds similar to the **o** in *"lot."* Example: **bò, fò, kò, lòt, nòt, pòt, sòt, wòch**.

CREOLE PHONETICS

Vowel	Pronunciation	Example
a	[ah]	like in water
e	[ey]	like in obey, not key
i	[ee]	like in fin
o	[oh]	like in go
è	[e]	like in let
ò	[o]	like in lot

- *An*, can be a difficult nasal to pronounce for English speakers; sounds like **an** in *"avant-garde"* with a silent *n*. Remember that **n** is silent in all of the following examples *an, ban, dan, danje, jan, nan san.*

- *En* sounds similar to the sound in *"sent"* but the *n* is silent. Example: *men, fent, gen, pen, ren, sen*. *Sent* is also a Kreyòl word and is a female Saint; the male Saint is *sen* and the **n** is silent, as it always is in a nasal. A critical word to familiarize yourself with is *mwen,* the first-person pronoun. It sounds similar to "when," but the ending *n* is silent. Don't worry if you cannot pronounce those blends perfectly at first; your pronunciation will improve with practice.

- *In* sounds similar to *een*. *Fin* is French, English, and Kreyòl and in Kreyòl it's pronounced like a shark fin, and not like "the end" in French. *Fin* is the abbreviated form of the verb *fini,* which means *"to finish."* Similarly, *vin* sounds similar to *fin;* it's the abbreviated form of the verb *vini,* which means "to come."

- *On* sounds similar to *"wont"* where *n* is silent. Example: *bon, bonbon, fon, fwon, kon, on, son, ton, won. Won* means *round* and the ending *n* is silent.

- *Ou* sounds like *oo* in pool. Example: *dous, douz, fou, goute, kou, mou, nou, ou, out, pou, poul, sou.*

NASALS & BLENDS

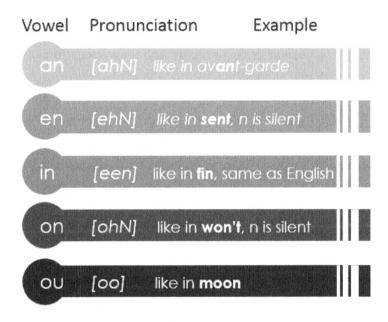

Vowel	Pronunciation	Example
an	[ahN]	like in av**an**t-garde
en	[ehN]	like in **sent**, n is silent
in	[een]	like in **fin**, same as English
on	[ohN]	like in **won't**, n is silent
ou	[oo]	like in **moon**

👁 Tip

English	Kreyòl
the	a [ah]
the	an [ahN]
to have	gen [gehN]
danger	danje [dahN-zhey]
I	mwen [mwehN]
to finish	fin [feen]
for	pou [poo]
strong, smart, must	fò [fo]
letter, milk	lèt [let]

While the following is not critical at this stage, you can achieve a highly authentic accent by making two key adjustments. The first is to shorten the sound that every letter or word makes. In English, we tend to prolong the ending sound of the letters. For example, the letter *c* pronounced in English sounds like the Kreyòl word *si*, while *d* pronounced in English sounds like the Kreyòl word *di*. Don't linger on the ending *ee* sound as you would in English. In Creole, do your best to shorten the sound, ending it briskly. This is applicable to every sound of every letter and word. Later, you will see words like *pat* and *bat*; you want to use the same principle by not prolonging the *ah* sound and instead ending it briskly. This is even more prevalent with the *e* that sounds like *ey*; the sound should end so suddenly that the *y* is not heard.

The second adjustment is to establish the proper position of your tongue when pronouncing *d*. In English, when pronouncing *d*, your tongue touches the roof of your mouth. In Creole, however, you need to move it to the edge of your teeth, as you do with the letter *c*. Try it and note the difference. By pronouncing *d* while touching your front teeth with your tongue, you pronounce the following homonyms perfectly in Creole: *"to say"* or *"to tell"* and *"hard"* or *"difficult."* The correct spelling in Kreyòl is *di*.

That's pretty much the bulk of what you need to know when it comes to pronunciation. Once you learn to pronounce the four vowels *a, e, i,* and *o,* the accented vowels *è* and *ò*, the nasals *an, en,* and *on*, and the blends *in* and *ou*, your pronunciation will improve greatly. And as you recognize them, you will be able to easily read Kreyòl. The majority of the words within this resource are words that are spelled the same in both languages; when you encounter them later on, you need to get used to pronouncing them in Kreyòl.

Given that Kreyòl is a phonetic language, the sounds never change. The phonetics you learn here never vary, remaining with you forever. You should now be able to read the sample sentences below. Because of the difficulty of mastering the pronunciation of a new language, one typically focuses on pronunciation last. However, the Kreglish methodology allows you to begin mastering pronunciation first.

To double-check your pronunciation, visit my YouTube channel: Haiti2030 @ https://tinyurl.com/yd7nb3gz where I post videos on various topics.

Tip

The text *[in italics and square brackets]* indicates how to pronounce the words. Note that *[hN]* h followed by capital **N** is always going to follow a vowel and it indicates a nasal with a silent n. **N** after a vowel is pronounced only in cases where there is a double **N**. Example: **Aprann**, which means "to learn."

Sample Sentences

I'm going to assume that you've mastered the pronunciations of the vowels, nasals, and the blend **ou**. Let's practice with the sentences below with brand new helper words that you'll need to recognize when a native speaker addresses you. For example, within the first sentence on the right-hand side, **se** is a new word. However, since you now know that consonant phonetics do not vary much between the two languages, you can deduce that the consonant **s** sounds the same as English, and as you just learned, the vowel **e** sounds likey **ey**, with the difference that **y** is silent. As a result, you can confidently pronounce **se**, which sounds like "*say*," but with a silent **y** and the overall sound shortened.

Meaning **Kreyòl spelling** (same pronunciation as cell to the right)	Read in English
They said that life is hard **Se yo ki di ke vi a di**	*Se* yo key D K V a D
They said that their lives are in danger **Yo di ke vi yo an danje**	Yo D K V yo an danje
Life is senseless **Vi a san sans**	V a san sans
She said that she isn't eating **Li di ke li pap manje**	Li D K li pap manje

He didn't say it **Se pa li ki te di sa**	Se pa li key te D sa
They don't know how to do it **Yo pa konn ki jan pou yo fè L**	Yo pa con key jan pou yo fell
I don't know what time I'm coming **Mwen pa konn a ki lè M ap vini**	Mwen pa con a key lè map vini
Life is hard **La vi a rèd**	La vi a red
I can't see the other one **Mwen pa ka wè lòt la**	Mwen pa ka wè lot la
I'm almost done saying what I had to say **Mwen prèske fin di sa M t ap di a**	Mwen press K fin D Sam tap D a

With the phonetics pretty much mastered, you can begin absorbing the vocabulary within to build a strong foundation. Mark or note the examples that contain the words you find most useful. Push through any nerves or awkwardness and start using them in your conversation. Just like exercising, you should practice what you're learning daily. That's the best way to continue making progress.

From this point forward, I'm confident that you can progress from the English words and expressions we've been using thus far and transition to using actual Kreyòl words. However, you'll notice that most of the words will continue to look familiar. The entire premise of this teaching methodology is to take advantage of the similarities between the two languages, a golden nugget that was hidden until my research led me to the following startling discovery: *pale* is an English word and a Kreyòl word, spelled identically. I later found that there are hundreds of words that fall in the same category. As I continued researching, I discovered that there also thousands of Kreyòl words and expressions that sound English; which is what we just covered. We'll continue to take advantage of those similarities to get you to engage in conversation as soon as possible.

3. Kreglish Explained

Over the next few pages, you'll begin reading and speaking Kreyòl without the use of the helper English words, but before we do so, I want to insure you have a good understanding of the Kreglish methodology and its benefits. I'll use the names of some celebrities I'm hoping you'll recognize. Depending on your age you may not know them all but trust me they were all celebrities at some point. I will place either their last name, nickname, or initials in what looks like a sentence, which you'll read as if you're reading a sentence. What you read will sound like a Kreyòl sentence. If you have a Kreyòl speaking friend next to you or one you can call on the phone, you can test the accuracy of this exercise by having them translate what you read to them. Ready? Let's do it.

Below is the sentence we're going to work with. The celebrities are: Bruce **Lee**, **Vinny** Testaverde, Shaquille O'Neal nicknamed **Shaq**, and **Sam D**onaldson.

> Lee Vinny Shaq Sam D **1**   Li vini chak samdi **2**

1 is English, which you can read
2 is Creole but, sounds just like 1
by reading 1, you spoke Creole
and said
He comes every Saturday

Although this is a relatively simple sentence, it's packed with lots of valuable information that's beneficial for you to get used to right away. The key to pronunciation lies in the sounds of the vowels and certain blends like the nasals. The sounds of the consonants aren't all that crucial because they don't vary much between the two languages. For now, let's analyze the Kreyòl sentence above and pay close attention to the vowels.

In the sentence **Li vini chak samdi**, there are only two vowels. If you compare that sentence to the grouping of the celebrities' names in terms of the way they're pronounced, you can deduce that the vowel *i* in *li* is pronounced [ee] like in Lee. We will make a small adjustment to the way you pronounce the vowel *a* in Sam; it's to be pronounced *[ah]* like in water.

35

There are four main vowels in the Kreyòl language; while the other two, *e* and *o,* weren't used in the sentence, I'll go ahead and cover them here as well. The vowel *"o"* is pronounced *[oh]* and *"e"* is pronounced *[ey]* in *obey,* not *key,* with the caveat that "y" is silent.

Vowel	Pronunciation
a	ah as the a in water or cafe
e	ey as the e in cafe or obey, not key
i	ee like in fin
o	o like in oh

The nice thing about this is that those sounds that we just covered and all sounds in Kreyòl for that matter are constant. We don't have the concept of long or short vowels. Every time you see any of those vowels, you need to pronounce them as we just did. It's crucial that you remember that piece of information that instantly enables you to read and pronounce thousands of Kreyòl words.

The following are the words to note and begin using at your earliest opportunity, in order to practice and retain what you learn. As much as you can, use the celebrities' names as memory aids. This is a very effective method for everything you learn throughout this resource. For example, if you want to refer another person as he or she, think of Bruce Lee's last name.

English	Kreyòl	Meaning
Lee	li	he, she or it
Vinny	vini	to come
Shaq	chak	every
Sam D	samdi	Saturday

Let's continue to build on that sentence and unveil some additional detail. We're going to move very quickly and then we'll slow back down to let you catch your breath. Let's get right into conjugation; don't worry I'm confident you can handle it. You'll get to explore conjugation in more detail in a later chapter. To continue to work on your pronunciation, take a look at these additional sentences below that you can also read. I'm adding a few additional words to the original sentence. They should also look familiar and they're pronounced similar to English words you're familiar with. The new words are **map, lap, nap** and **yap**. Do you think you can handle those? In addition to those three, we'll also throw in **wap**; although the latter isn't an actual English word, it has the same structure and should be pronounced the same as the others above. Our new sentences look like this:

Rea in English	Kreyòl Spelling	Meaning
Map Vinny Shaq Sam D	**M** ap vini chak samdi	**I**'m coming every Saturday
Wap Vinny Shaq Sam D	**W** ap vini chak samdi	**You**'re coming every Saturday
Lap Vinny Shaq Sam D	**L** ap vini chak samdi	**He**'s coming every Saturday
Nap Vinny Shaq Sam D	**N** ap vini chak samdi	**We**'re coming every Saturday
Nap Vinny Shaq Sam D	**N** ap vini chak samdi	**You**'re coming every Saturday
Yap Vinny Shaq Sam D	**Y** ap vini chak samdi	**They**'re coming every Saturday

Congratulations you just conjugated the verb **vini**, which means *"to come"* in the progressive form or future tense, without breaking a sweat. How easy was that? The first and second column are pronounced pretty much the same. Even though there's a space after the first letter in the second column, the space is to be ignored when reading the sentence. **M** & **ap** are pronounced as a single word that sounds like *[map]*; the only adjustment is to continue to pronounce **a** *[ah]* like in water. This form is used when the abbreviated pronoun is followed by a verb or modal helper word that begins with a vowel. In this example, the abbreviated pronoun is placed before the verb as a subject, but it could also be placed after the verb as a complement, in which case it's also pronounced along with the word that precedes it. For example, **fè L** is pronounced *[fell]* and means *"do it"* while **pa M** is pronounced *[Pam]* and means "mine". As we indicated earlier, the **a** in Pam is pronounced *[ah]*.

Tip

Every pronoun has an abbreviated form; which is a single letter word similar to *I* in English; the Kreyòl abbreviated pronouns are also capitalized. This is not a Kreyòl standard, but it is a format I adopted to differentiate from the other one-letter words that aren't pronouns.

M, W, L, N, N, and Y are the abbreviated forms the pronouns

The Pronouns		
	Singular	**Plural**
First Person	Mwen *[mwehN]* *M*	Nou *[noo]* N
Second Person	Ou *[oo]* *W*	Nou *[noo]* N
Third Person	Li *[lee]* *L*	Yo *[yoh]* Y

Let's go back to our celebrity sentence: Li vini chak samdi, drop the word ***chak*** to keep things simple and set up some complete conjugation tables.

Translation	You can read this and it sounds Creole
I'm coming on Saturday	M ap vini Samdi
You're coming on Saturday	W ap vini Samdi
He's coming on Saturday	L ap vini Samdi
We're coming on Saturday	N ap vini Samdi
You're coming on Saturday	N ap vini Samdi
They're coming on Saturday	Y ap vini Samdi

Now that you know the pronouns let's slightly modify the original sentence to show you how easy it is to conjugate verbs in Kreyòl.

Present Tense

English	Kreyòl
I come	Mwen vini
You come	Ou vini

He/she comes	Li vini
We come	Nou vini
You come	Nou vini
They come	Yo vini

Below is a series of words that you are familiar with; each of these words is a Kreyòl verb; since you had plenty of practice pronouncing the vowels, you should try to pronounce these verbs without looking back at the vowel pronunciation chart.

English	Kreyòl Verbs
to go	ale, al (abbreviation)
to leave, let	kite
to speak	pale
to sweep	bale

I invite you to practice aloud by replacing the verb *vini* with each of the verbs in the above table. Let's now take a look at the word *ap*, which is a modal helper word, pronounced *[app]*. In Kreyòl we don't have the concept of modal auxiliary verbs like *to be* or *to have*; we instead have a series of short words that mark the progressive form, past tense, conditional, and others. I call them modal helper words. Let's take a look at some and add them to our original sentence along with the new verbs we just introduced.

Function	Modal helper Words
future tense or progressive form	ap *[ahp]*
past tense	te *[tey]*
not yet	poko, pako *[poh-koh]*
not (negative sentence)	pa *[pah]*

Right now, it's okay to use either the full or the abbreviated form of the pronouns. As you become more proficient, you'll learn which one is more appropriate. The rule of thumb is that if the verb or modal helper word starts with a consonant, the full form is used; if the verb or modal helper word starts with a vowel, the abbreviated form is used. Let's take a look at some very easy conjugation exercises.

Present Tense

English	Kreyòl
I go	M ale
You go	W ale
He/she goes	L ale
We go	N ale
You go	N ale
They go	Y ale

Past Tense

English	Kreyòl
I swept	Mwen te bale
You swept	Ou te bale
He/she swept	Li te bale
We swept	Nou te bale
You swept	Nou te bale
They swept	Yo te bale

Negative Sentence

English	Kreyòl
I don't speak Creole	Mwen pa pale Kreyòl
You don't speak Creole	Ou pa pale Kreyòl
He/she doesn't speak Creole	Li pa pale Kreyòl
We don't speak Creole	Nou pa pale Kreyòl
You don't speak Creole	Nou pa pale Kreyòl
They don't speak Creole	Yo pa pale Kreyòl

Use of Not Yet

English	Kreyòl
I haven't left yet	Mwen poko kite
You haven't left yet	Ou poko kite

He/she hasn't left yet	Li poko kite
We haven't left yet	Nou poko kite
You haven't left yet	Nou poko kite
They haven't left yet	Yo poko kite

In keeping with the theme that the majority of words in this resource are spelled like a familiar English word, I present to you some additional verbs that follow the same pattern. In the case of the verbs *prepare* & *vote*, they're perfect cognates, where the meaning and spelling are the same in both languages. The pronunciation is such that the ending **e** is pronounced, keeping in mind that **e** is always pronounced *[ey]*, **a** is always pronounced *[ah]*, and **o** is always pronounced *[oh]*.

English	Kreyòl
to be ready	pare
to finish	fin (abbreviation of fini)
to prepare	prepare
to step on	pile
to swallow	vale
to sweat	transpire
to tie down	mare
to vote	vote

4- Relate to Remember

When I told my student Kate that I planned to teach her Kreyòl using English words, she was skeptical. She didn't understand how learning a series (**seri**) of random words could help her become fluent in the language. Kate already knew a lot of Kreyòl and was a passionate (**pasyone**) learner, which is probably the most crucial attribute required to learn a new language. I explained to her that she was the prime student for my methodology and that it would help her immensely, especially (**espesyalman**) with pronunciation and memorization. With simple (**senp**) concepts like recognizing the cognates, along with passion (**pasyon**), she could fully take advantage (**avantaj**) of this innovative way of learning Kreyòl, a method (**metòd**) that can possibly be adapted to learn other languages, too (**tou**).

Once I introduced (**entwodui**) the **R2R** method to Kate, the rest (**rès**) was history. This language learning technique (**teknik**) uses the power of association (**asosyasyon**) to greatly increase your ability to memorize (**memorize**) and apply vocabulary (**vokabilè**). Once you can relate to something, it becomes easier to remember. I've been able to remember many words and expressions (**ekspresyon**) I learned many moons ago from a variety of languages (**lang**) by applying R2R.

Here is how it works: if you teach me a new word or expression (**ekspresyon**) in Korean for example, I cannot write nor read it, but I can hear it. And if whatever I hear sounds like Kreyòl,

English, or anything else in my environment (**anviwonman**), I can guarantee (**garanti**) you I will retain it for good.

Kreyòl has a large number of short words. As a result, a large number of the acronyms you're already familiar with are spelled exactly (**egzakteman**) like some pretty common Kreyòl words. You can add these to your vocabulary right away. The trick (**trik**) is to associate (**asosye**) the Kreyòl word below with the acronym or anything else that can help you remember it; the acronym is merely a suggested relationship (**relasyon**) to help memorization.

Kreyòl / Acronym	R2R / Memory Aid	English
ak *[ack]*	alaska	with
ap *[ahp]*	associated press	-ing form (progressive)
avè *[ah-ve]*	ave (avenue)	with
eta *[ey-tah]*	estimated time of arrival	state
pa *[pah]*	physician assistant	not
pap *[pahp]*	pap smear	will not
pe *[pey]*	physical education	to shut up
pi *[pee]*	π: 3.1416	more
sa *[sah]*	south america	this, that
ta *[tah]*	teacher's assistant	late
te *[tey]*	the end	past tense
ti *[tee]*	tiny insect	little, small

Personally, these are the relationships I would create to help me remember these new words.

- For the word *ap [app]*, I suggest that you create the following relationship (**relasyon**): "The Associated Press is always writ**ING** and report**ING**". By making a mental (**mantal**) note (**nòt**) of that sentence with the two verbs (**vèb**) ending in -*ing*, I'm sure you'll be able to retain its definition (**definisyon**).

- For *pa [pah]*, I suggest (**sigjere**) you make a mental note of the following sentence: A physician assistant is **NOT** a doctor.

- For *pi [pee]*: There are many **MORE** digits after the decimal point in *Pi* (π) than those that are usually displayed.

- For *ti* [*tee*]: think Tiny Insect - **SMALL**.

  The following examples are my favorite R2R associations:

- *Ale* [*Ah-ley*] means "*to go*" in Kreyòl, but in English it is a type (**tip**) of beer (**byè**). This is how we can use R2R for this word: When you drink beer, you **GO** to the restroom constantly.

- *Kite* [*kee-tey*] means to leave or let go. A kite is a toy that you **LET GO** up in the air.

- *Vini* [vee-nee] means "*to come*," and it is pronounced (**pwononse**) just like the Italian male (**mal**) name Vinny. If you are not familiar with that name, one famous (**fame**) Vinny is Vinny Testaverde who used to be a quarterback in the NFL. You could also picture an imaginary (**imajinè**) friend named Vinny, whose family **CAME** from Italy to the US a long (**long**) time ago.

- *Sou* [*soo*] sounds like "*sue*" and it means "on." You may remember that meaning by making the following connection (**koneksyon**). When you file a lawsuit against someone, you are **ON** that person's case, meaning you are all over that person.

- *Dan* [*dahN*] means "*tooth*." Do you know anyone named Dan? Maybe it's a neighbor, your real estate agent, or a high school classmate, better yet a dentist. Was there anything special about his teeth? If not, imagine you know Dan the dentist who has the whitest **TEETH** you have ever seen.

There's a medical (**medikal**) and dental (**dantal**) mission (**misyon**) at my church in Duluth, GA that goes to Hinche, Haiti, three times a year. Jim is a successful orthodontist who has been going on the mission trip for more than twenty years. Once when I helped the team with language training, I asked Jim if he knew how to say *tooth* in Kreyòl. After dozens (**douzèn**) of trips over twenty years, there are so many patients to see during the weeklong trips that Jim and others like him find it difficult (**difisil**) to make time for language training. On top of that, there is the misconception (**miskonsepsyon**) that learning any foreign language is a mountain to climb. My objective (**objektif**) is to debunk that myth. I do so by using techniques such as R2R, which is put to use in this last scenario (**senaryo**) to engrave (**grave**) the word **dan** in Jim's memory (**memwa**), a word that's so vital for a dentist (**dantis**).

Kreyòl offers many more opportunities (**opòtinite**) like the above, in which its similarity to English allows for the formation of easy mnemonic devices. When learning a new Kreyòl word, if you can associate it with something you are familiar with, the likelihood of retention is much higher than if you just drilled vocabulary without R2R.

 Tip

Long is written and pronounced the same in both languages. It also has the same meaning. Although many words are spelled the same across the two languages, it is rare that they are pronounced the same and have the same meaning. *Long* is one of the rare exceptions.

Of course, R2R is not nearly as effective when someone else is making the associations for you. Forming your own R2R associations from life experiences is the most effective way to memorize vocabulary. Don't be afraid to have fun and get creative with it! There is one caveat: Don't try to use this technique (**teknik**) on too many words at once (at least not at the beginning). If you do, you risk mixing up your associations. Try to stick to smaller vocabulary sets until you feel more comfortable (**konfòtab**) increasing the number of words.

As you learn Kreyòl words and memorize their meanings using R2R, you can then begin working on recognizing these words in context. Though you might not understand everything spoken in a conversation or written in an article or book, you can pick up on key words, and in many cases you'll be able to understand what you hear or read without knowing all the words in a sentence or conversation.

Sample Sentences

Use the sentences below to practice pronunciation aloud and to learn to recognize words that you've already encountered, such as the ones covered in the R2R section.

English	Kreyòl
This food is very tasty	Manje sa a gou anpil
The coffee is good	Kafe a bon
She and her kid have the same disease	Li gen menm maladi a pitit li a
The airplane won't arrive on time	Avyon an pap rive a lè
I am not happy that you left without me	M pa kontan ke W al kite M
She will never let you go	Li pap janm kite W ale
The president said he did not inhale	Prezidan an di li pa t aspire
She won't let the car go	Li pap kite machin nan ale
She won't leave without me	Li pap ale san mwen

Between Haiti and the United States, where would you prefer to be right now?	Ant Ayiti ak Eta Zini, ki bò ou ta pi renmen ye kounyè a?
The road is long	Wout la long
I'm going to go see my dentist	Mwen pwal wè dantis mwen an
The dentist cleaned my teeth	Dantis la te netwaye dan M
Nothing is wrong with your teeth	Ou pa gen anyen nan dan
Today we'll only clean your teeth	Jodi a N ap annik netwaye dan W

5- The Pronouns (Pwonon Yo)

It's important to revisit the pronouns and conjugation and share some additional details that would have been premature to introduce earlier. Contrary to English, wherein we find multiple pronoun types (personal, possive, reflexive, and intensive, etc.), Kreyòl only uses one pronoun. In the case of the possessive pronouns, *pou* precedes the pronoun if the full form is used and *pa* if it's the abbreviated form. For example, *pou mwen* and *pa M* are used interchangeably and mean "*mine.*" The same holds true for all the other pronouns except for the third person plural where the full form **yo** is used with either **pou** or **pa**.

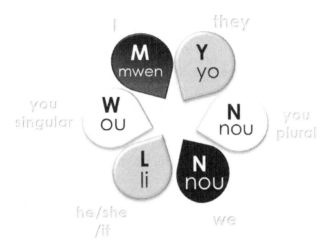

Folks who are introduced (**entwodui**) to English for the first time, sometimes get confused by *you* singular (**sengilye**) and *you* plural (**pliryèl**), in terms of figuring out which is which. We encounter (**rankontre**) a similar situation (**sitiyasyon**) in Creole because the first- and second-person plural are both *nou*. Over time you'll be able to recognize (**rekonèt**) which is being used, but one rule of thumb that is that if you ask a question (**kesyon**), you typically aren't included in the group of people you're referring to; therefore you are asking others and referring to the second person plural. However, if you're stating something, you typically include yourself and it's the first-person plural.

In all but one case (**ka**), the abbreviated form (**fòm**) of the pronouns is the first letter (**lèt**) of the full word. The exception (**eksepsyon**) is the second person singular *ou*, where the abbreviated form is *W*. The abbreviated form is used when the preceding word ends with a vowel (**vwayèl**) or a nasal sound (**son**) or when the succeeding word, usually a verb or a modal helper word begins with a vowel.

The abbreviation can either precede the verb (**vèb**) in a subjective case (**ka**) or it can follow the verb in an objective case. There are two special (**espesyal**) cases to the above rule. The abbreviated form of the first person, **M,** is the only one that is allowed to precede a verb that starts with a consonant. And the abbreviated form, **Y** of the third person plural is never used in an objective case; the full form **yo** is always used. **Pa egzanp**:

I understand	**Mwen konprann** or **M konprann**
I told them	**Mwen pale yo** or **M pale yo**

Using R2R, you can easily remember all of the pronouns. As stated earlier, it is best for you to come up with your own relationships (**relasyon**), as this will greatly enhance retention. However, in the case of the pronouns, I've discovered some highly effective mnemonics that I'm happy to share with you.

In analyzing the first person singular **mwen**, you will see the word *men* with an added **w**. That's the clue I offer (**ofri**) you to help you memorize the pronoun **mwen**.

I am done speaking	**Mwen fin pale**
Let me go	**Kite M ale**

Ou translates to "*you.*" An easy application of R2R in this case is to think of the pronoun **ou** as *you* without the *y*.

You can leave without them	**Ou mèt ale kite yo**

Similarly, **nou**, the first- and second-person plural, which translates to *we* as well as *you* plural, is *you* with an **n** instead of **y**.

We removed it	**Nou retire L**
Did you all prepare it?	**Ès ke nou prepare L?**

Li, the third person singular sounds just like Lee and is gender neutral. It also refers to people as well as objects.

He gave me a (piece of) bread   **Li ban mwen on pen**

In this example, it is more appropriate to use the abbreviated form of the pronoun *mwen,* resulting in **Li ban M on pen.**

Yo, the slang English word, is the third person plural "they."
They adore him   **Yo adore L**

Note the word choice in the above examples: **fin, pale, adore, pen ban, retire, prepare, on, ale, kite** are all Kreyòl words with the same spelling as some English words that you know. Although their meanings and pronunciations are different, you already know how to spell them.

Object Pronouns

Objects pronouns are used so that object nouns are not continuously repeated. In English the object pronouns *me, you, his / her / it, us,* and *them* are different from the subject pronouns. However, they're the same in Kreyòl and both the full and abbreviated forms are also used. Just like in the case of the subject pronouns, the ending of the preceding verb determines whether the full or abbreviated form is used. In the case of the third person plural, the full form **yo** is always used.

In Kreyòl, the abbreviated pronouns and all other single-letter words are considered extensions of the accompanying words that they precede or succeed. A single letter word is not to be pronounced like the letter of the alphabet. Its behavior in terms of pronunciation is similar to that of the plural mark **s** or the apostrophe followed by s in English. Whether it precedes or succeeds the word it modifies, the single letter word and the accompanying word run onto each other in terms of sound. For example, *Di M*, which means "*tell me*," is similar in pronunciation to the English word *[dim],* and **Si M**, which means "*if I*", sounds ver much like *[seem].*

Fè L means "*do it.*" Its pronunciation is similar to *[fell]*; this is very common as the verb *fè*, which means "*to do*" is widely used in Kreyòl. There is a running joke about some words that are overused in Kreyòl. **Fè** is one of those words. *Di L*, which means "*tell him or her*" is the abbreviated form of **di li** and is pronounced just like *[dill]*. **Di** is one of the first verb we learned at the beginning as one of the letters of the alphabet that sounds like a Kreyòl word. Below are a couple of example sentences.

We all adore him	**Nou tout adore L**
They did it	**Se yo ki fè L**
He's the one who said it	**Se li ki di L**
She carried all of them	**Li pote yo tout**
She gave me hers	**Li ban M pa L yo**
She let us go	**Li kite N ale**

Once you master the use of the Kreyòl pronouns, your ability to construct more sophisticated, grammatically correct sentences will increase exponentially. From this point, we will operate under the assumption that you can recognize the pronouns without any assistance.

Possessive pronouns

The possessive pronouns mine, yours, his, hers, ours, and theirs are used to replace a possessive adjective and noun. The Kreyòl possessive pronouns consist of the word **pou** followed by the full form of the pronouns or the word **pa** followed by the abbreviated form of the pronouns. There's only one exception, in the case of the third person plural, it's always the full form of the pronoun **yo**, just like we saw earlier for the object pronoun

Possessive Pronouns				
	Singular		**Plural**	
First Person	**pou mwen** *pa M*	mine	**pou nou** **pa N**	ours
Second Person	**pou ou** **pa W**	yours	**pou nou** **pa N**	yours
Third Person	**pou li** **pa L**	his / hers	**pou yo** **pa yo**	theirs

Pa M means "mine." Its pronounciation is similar to *[Pam]*, or more accurately, *[pahm]*. *Pa W*, which means means "*yours*" is the abbreviated form of **pa ou** and is pronounced similar to the sound made in [cow]. If you were to use the full form of the pronoun, it would be **pou ou**. *or more precisely [paht]*. As a final example, *Pa L*, pronounced *[pal] or more precisely [pahl]*, means "his or hers." Below are a couple of example sentences.

This one isn't mine	**Sa a pa pou mwen**
Mine's the best	**Pa M nan pi bon**
She gave me hers	**Li ban M pa L yo**
Yours is newer	**Pa W la pi nèf**

As a possessive or object pronoun, the third-person singular that translates to **li** or **L** the majority of the time, is also **ni** or **N** when the preceding sound in a nasal. For example we say:

| She put **her** foot on me | Li met pye **L** sou mwen |

On the other hand we say:

| She put her hand on my back | Li met men **N** sou do M |

In the first sentence, the third-person singular is **L**, the abbreviated form of **li** and in the second, we use **N**, the abbreviated form of **ni**. Below are some additional example sentences.

They gave it to me	**Yo ban M ni**
I'm the one who took it	**Se mwen k pran N**
They sold it for lots of money	**Yo vann ni pou anpil kòb**
I'll bring it to you	**M ap mennen N ba ou**
That's her man	**Se nonm ni**
That's his girl	**Se fanm ni**
Take it for me	**Pran N pou mwen**
Wait for her at the park	**Ret tann ni sou plas la**

WORD SEARCH

The word search below will test your knowledge of some common words you've seen earlier. In the table at the bottom of the page the English word is given, please circle the Kreyòl equivalent. Hint: in most cases the Kreyòl and English words are the same; in the remaining cases the Kreyòl equivalent is spelled the same as an English word with a different meaning.

E	R	I	P	S	N	A	R	T	E	E	V
F	Z	L	V	S	P	L	A	N	R	S	F
E	R	I	M	D	A	H	R	O	A	O	F
I	K	V	R	R	B	L	D	R	P	U	D
G	O	O	E	O	D	A	A	O	E	P	N
N	O	B	V	T	M	I	N	D	R	V	A
O	I	M	L	E	E	E	L	K	P	I	M
L	C	A	Q	E	R	R	M	O	D	T	E
R	E	S	P	I	R	E	A	P	S	A	D
E	T	O	V	N	P	L	A	N	T	M	R
Q	Q	N	H	C	T	A	M	F	L	I	V
L	U	Z	Y	O	P	R	U	L	U	N	P

TO ADMIRE	TO ADORE	BANK
TO DEMAND	LIBERAL	LONG
MASON	MATCH	TO MEMORIZE
PLAN	PLANT	TO PREPARE
TO RESPIRE	TO REVOKE	SALAD
SOLID	SOUP	TO TRANSPIRE
VETERAN	VITAMIN	TO VOTE

Part II

Grammar

5- Single-Letter Words

The English language has two single-letter words: *I* and *a*. In comparison (**konparezon**), Kreyòl has many more. In addition (**adisyon**) to the abbreviated form of the pronouns that we saw earlier, *M, W, L, N, and Y*, there also are:

- **A** – a word shared by both languages. It has several meanings in Kreyòl: "the," "with," the exclamation "ah," it's sometimes placed after **la** like in **la a**, in which case it means "there" or after **sa** like in **sa a** and means "this or that."
- **E** – means "and," "plus" or "how about."
- **È** – means "air" it's also used to tell time.
- **K** – short for *ki*, means "who" or "what**."**
- **O** – is the exclamation "oh**."**
- **T** – short for *te*, defines the past tense.

The chart and table that follow contain a list of single-letter Kreyòl words along with their English translations. Just like I in English, I capitalize the abbreviated form of all pronouns. I wish this was a standard, but as of this writing I don't believe it is. It's just the convention I personally adopt in my writing.

Single Letter Words – Except for A, E, & O, the majority of the single letter words are abbreviations with half of them being the abbreviated form of the pronouns.

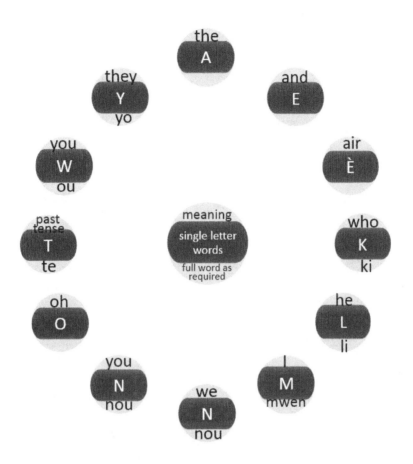

He's coming with his sister	**L ap vini a sè L la**
How about the kids?	**E ti moun you?**
He didn't know	**Li pa t konnen**
The AC is cold	**È kondisyone a frèt**
What's happening?	**Sa k ap fèt?**
Oh, I see!	**O, M wè!**
Put this one in the same spot	**Mete sa a nan menm plas la**
They'll give it to you	**Y ap ba W li**
They're the ones who told us	**Se yo k di N**
Ah, I understand	**A, M konprann**

Words	Full Word where applicable	English
a	a *[ah]*	the, with, ah
e	e *[ey]*	and, plus, how about
è	e [e]	air, o'clock
k	ki *[kee]*	who, that
L	li *[lee]*	he / she / it
M	mwen *[mwehN]*	I
N	nou *[noo]*	we
N	nou *[noo]*	you
o	o *[oh]*	oh
t	te *[tey]*	past tense
W	ou *[oo]*	you
Y	yo *[yoh]*	they

6- Cognates & Substitutes

Before we go any further, let us take a look at some words you may have a hard time recognizing at first. After a few examples, I have no doubt it will become easier for you to begin recognizing them and others like them. By developing the ability to recognize the cognates, you will begin building the vocabulary needed for Kreyòl fluency.

The word **Kreyòl** itself is loaded with several substitution rules. The first rule is that the hard **c** sound is always represented by the letter **k**, the second one is the use of **y** between the two vowels **e** and **ò**. *In Kreyòl two vowels follow each other only in the following two cases: **ou** & **ui**. When dealing with cognates, everywhere two vowels follow each other in English, **y** is slotted in between them in Kreyòl; and if **i** precedes the second vowel, it's replaced with **y**. Pa egzanp "creation" means* **kreyasyon**. In this example, you should also note a very common substitution rule; the entire **tion** ending in English is replaced with **syon**. Note some of the most common substitutions in the table below.

English	Kreyòl Substitute	Example
-able	-ab	table - tab
-ary	-è	contrary - kontrè
-c (soft c sound)	always s	patience - pasyans
-c / ch that sound like k and q / qu	always k	echo - eko
con / com followed by b or p	kon	to consider - konsidere
-en	-an	difference - diferans
-ible	-ib	terrible - terib
in / im followed by b or p	en	important - enpòtan
-ly	-man	clearly - klèman
-er	è	supporter - sipòtè
-or	-ò	comfort - konfò
-s that sounds like z	always z	reason - rezon
-tial / tiel	-syèl	potential - potansyèl
-tion	-syon	situation - sitiyasyon
-u between two consonants	i	music - mizik
-x	-gz / ks	maximum - maksimòm
-cc	-s / ks	accident - aksidan
-r before a consonant	omitted	market - makèt

While you add the common words below, see if you can recognize the different substitutions that are applied.

English	Kreyòl
accident	aksidan [ahk-see-dahN]
actor	aktè [ahk-te]
ambition	anbisyon [ahN-bee-tiohN]
cathedral	katedral [kah-tay-drahl]
to combine	konbine [koNh-bee-ney]
crime	krim [kreem]
echo	Eko [ey-koh]
elephant	elefan [ey-la-fahN]
esercise	egzèsis [ey-gze-sees]
favor	favè [fah-ve]
governor	gouvènè [goo-ve-ne]
hospital	lopital [loh-pee-tahl]
hotel	otèl / lotèl [loh-tel]
idea	ide [ee-dey]
important	enpòtan [en-po-tahN]
information	enfòmasyon [ehN-faw-mah-syohN]
to invent	envante [ehN-vahN-tey]
local	lokal [loh-kahl]
material	materyèl [mah-tey-ree-el]
motor	motè [moh-te]
music	mizik [mee-zeek]
natural	natirèl [nah-tee-rel]
photo	foto [foh-toh]
popular	popilè [poh-pee-le]
to present	prezante [prey-zahN-tey]
president	prezidan [prey-zee-dahN]
presidential	prezidansyèl [prey-zee-dahN-see-el]
radio	radyo [rah-dee-oh]
responsible	responsab [rey-spohN-sahb]

senator	senatè *[sey-nah-te]*
to support	sipòte *[see-po-tey]*
supporter	sipòtè *[see-po-te]*
tax	taks *[tahx]*
taxi	taksi *[tahk-see]*
telephone	telefòn *[tey-ley-fo-N]*

There are a few substitutions that require further explanation:

- *Or* is most of the time replaced with *ò*, especially in the middle of a word as opposed to the end. Pa egzanp, *"morn"* is **mòn**, *"force"* is **fòs**. **R** after a vowel is never pronounced along with the preceding vowel; it's rather pronounced along with the vowel that follows, and it's always a vowel. For example: **zoranj** *[zoh-rahN-zh]* means *"orange."* If **r** precedes a consonant in English, it's completely omitted in Kreyòl as you see in the first two examples of this paragraph: **mòn** & **fòs**.

- *R* before *o* is substituted with *w* when *r* is the first letter of the word or if it's preceded by a consonant. Pa egzanp: *"Program"* is **pwogram**, *"proverb"* is **pwovèb**, *"to protect"* is **pwoteje**, *"round"* is **won**, and *"route"* is **wout**.

- A double consonant is replaced with a single consonant as you can see in supporter (**sipòtè**). Double consonants are quite common in English. In Kreyòl there's only one letter that is sometimes doubled; that's *n* and its doubling is quite rare. Remember a while ago we mentioned that the ending *n* of the nasals is always silent. There are some words where you want the *n* to sound; those are the cases where we double the *n*. Pa egzanp, **tann** means *"to wait,"* **kann** means **"sugar cane,"** **sann** means *"ash,"* **venn** ,pronounced *[van]* means *"vein,"* and **konn** *[con]* is the abbreviated form of **konnen** and it means *"to know."*

- *In or im* followed by *b* or *p* make a sound similar to the Kreyòl *[ehN]* sound and they are replaced with *en*. Pa egzanp, *"imbecile"* is **enbesil**, *"simple"* is **senp**, and *"principle"* is **prensip**.

7- English and Kreyòl Words with the Same Spelling but Different Meanings

The vast majority of words used in this resource are identical in spelling to some English words you are familiar with, but have different meanings and pronunciations. Here is a subset below with the most common in bold face:

A	An	Ale	Ban
Bank	Dan	Do	**Fin**
Final	Foul	Gate	**Kite**
Long	**Men**	**Met**	On
Pale	Pen	Pike	Plan

Using the above words, very few practical English sentences can be formulated. However, several perfectly constructed Kreyòl sentences are within reach. For example, let us combine the following in a variety of ways: *met, pale,* and *kite*. You likely cannot think of too many English sentences to construct using these words, but when it comes to Creole, we have a lot of choices.

Kite M ale	Let me go
Ale kite M	Go without me
Kite M pale	Let me speak
Ou ka kite L pale	You may let him speak
Ès ke ou ka kite yo pale?	Can you let them speak
Ou mèt kite yo pale	You can let them speak

Again, combining *do, men,* and *met* in English will result in an incoherent sentence, but in Creole we get:

Li met men L sou do M	She put her hand on my back

Combining **Ban**, **gate**, **on**, and **pen** results in:

Li ban M on pen gate   He gave me some spoiled bread

Finally, combining **Dan**, **fin**, **gate**, and **yo** results in:

Dan W yo fin gate   Your teeth have gone bad

8- Rules for Indicating Gender and Plural

A major difference between the two languages deals with gender and plural. Gender plays an important role in the French language; however even with its close relationship to French, Kreyòl only has a handful of words that have a masculine and feminine version. Creole pronouns do not discriminate according to gender either; the pronoun *li [lee]* that we saw earlier is both masculine and feminine. Below are some of the few words with a feminine version.

Good day: **bon** jou (masculine usage)
Happy birthday: **bòn fèt** (feminine usage)
Cousin: **kouzen** (masculine), **kouzin** (feminine)
Neighbor: **vwazen** (masculine), **vwazin** (feminine)
Boss: **patwon** (masculine), **patwòn** (feminine)
Haitian: **Ayisyen** (masculine), **Ayisyèn** (feminine)
Crazy: **fou** (masculine), **fòl** (feminine)
Fresh: **fre** (masculine), **frèch** (feminine)
Next: **pwochen** (masculine), **pwochèn** (feminine)

In certain cases, although the masculine exists, the feminine version is used almost exclusively. In those cases, if the masculine is used, that's often referred to a French-like Kreyòl. Similarly, the feminine version of these adjectives isn't used to match the noun that's technically genderless.

Dry: **Sèk** (masculine), **Sèch** (feminine)
Beautiful: **Bo** (masculine), **Bèl** (feminine)
Ugly: L**èd** (feminine)
Dumb or not smart: **Sòt** (feminine)

As with gender, nouns and adjectives do not change to reflect a singular or plural form. In general, adding the letter *s* to certain words, as it is done in English, will change the identity of the word completely. This is best illustrated using words that are similar in spelling to English words. Pa egaznp:

Men means "hand" while **mens** means "thin"
Woman means "romantic novel," while **womans** means "romance"
Pan means "peacock" while **pans** means "intestine"

Ma means "residue" while **mas** means "March"

Mè means "mother" or "old lady" while **mès** means "mass" (church)

Pò means "port" while **pòs** means "post"

Ra means "rare" while **ras** means "race"

Ran means "row" while **rans** means "stale" in terms of tase

San means "without" or "blood" while **sans** means "sense"

Dan means "tooth" while **dans** means "dance"

Vi means "life" while **vis** means "vice" or "screw"

Good day	**Bonjou**
Happy birthday	**Bòn fèt**
He's coming next week	**L ap vini semèn pwochèn**
Yes, the vegetables are fresh	**Wi, legim yo frèch**
He's a handsone boy	**Li bo gason**
Lady, you have a beautiful child	**Madanm, ou gen on bèl pitit**
Without you, life is senseless	**San ou, vi a pa gen sans**
Excuse me, where's the post office?	**Eskize M, ki kote la pòs la ye?**
Don't judge peopled based on race	**Pa jije moun daprè ras yo**
We're getting married in March	**N ap marye an Mas**
She goes to mass every Sunday	**L al la mès chak Dimanch**
It's rare to see any peacocks in Haiti	**Li ra pou N wè pan an Ayiti**
The vice president is visiting the UN	**Vis prezidan an ap vizite Nasyon Zini**

9- Abbreviations

Many Creole words have abbreviated forms. I purposely use both the full word and the abbreviated form throughout this resource to get you used to both. With very few exceptions, both the full word and the abbreviation are used interchangeably. In addition to the pronouns that we saw earlier, below are several common abbreviated words.

Abbreviation	Full Word	Meaning
a, ak, avè	avèk [ah-vehk]	with
fin	fini [fee-nee]	to finish
konn	konnen [kohN-nehN]	to know
kot	kote [koh-tey]	side, where
met	mete [koh-tey]	to put
pot	pote [poh-tey]	to carry
ret	rete [ra-tey]	to stay
sot	soti [soh-tee]	to go out
tounen	retounen [rey-too-nehN]	to come back
vin	vini [vee-nee]	to come

She likes rice with beans	**Li renmen di ri a pwa**
Where is the doctor?	**Kot doktè a?**
Put your clothes on	**Met rad ou sou ou**
She came back withouth the kids	**Li tounen san ti moun yo**
Wait for me	**Ret tann mwen**
She's done with the surgery	**Li fin fè operasyon an**
She just came out of the operating room	**Li fèk sot nan sal operasyon an**

10- Names or Nicknames that are Spelled like Kreyòl Words

There are many English proper names and nicknames that are spelled identically to some Creole words. This is yet another case in which you already know the words and just need to learn how to appropriate them to Creole.

From this point forward, you will need to begin practicing your newly acquired Creole pronunciation. When you encounter words that look English, you need to remember that they are also Creole and need to be pronounced in Creole. To enable you to compose some more complex sentences, you'll also need to learn some helper words. We begin with the set of words below that are short, sweet and easy to remember. Most of them should also look familiar as they have identical spelling to some common English names or nicknames: *Al, dan, jan, jodi, kat, Kay, Mo, pa, pa m, pa t,* and *sal*.

Proper Name / Nickname	Pronunciation	Meaning
Al	al *[ahl]**	to go
Dan	dan *[dahN]*	tooth
Fran	fran *[frahN]*	frank
Jan	jan *[jahN]*	manner, way
Jodi	jodi a *[zhoh-dee-ah]*	today
Kat	kat *[kaht]*	four, card
Kay	kay *[kah y]*	house
Kim	kim *[keem]*	suds (soap)
Mo	mo *[moh]*	word
Pam	pa M *[pahm]*	mine
Pat	pat *[paht]*	dough
Pat	pa t *[paht]*	didn't
Pete	pete *[pey-tey]*	to fart
Sal	sal *[sahl]*	dirty, room
Wes	wès *[wes]*	west
Zak	zak *[zahk]*	actions

One of the sentences we saw early on was about a group of kids whose lives are hard. You now know enough to compose similar sentences in the negative form using newly learned words that are common to both languages. In that scenario, we used the letters *c, d, t, and v,* and the words *con* and *Vinny* as they are written and pronounced in English. Instead of using the letters as we did earlier, we now use the words that I'm sure you are able to recognize and pronounce.

She stayed at the house alone	**Li ret nan kay la pou kont li**
They don't know how to say it	**Yo pa konn ki jan pou yo di L**
Today is the day we clean the house	**Jodi a se jou pou N netwaye kay la**
She only said four words	**Li di kat mo sèlman**

The following are some additional English-sounding words that can be very useful for your continued improvement in terms of pronunciation. Pay close attention to the vowel sounds and pretty soon you'll have no need for the pronunciation keys provided.

Kreyòl Pronunciation	Kreyòl	Meaning
app	ap	-ing form or future tense
bow (like in bow down)	ba w	give you
bush	bouch	mouth
diss	dis	ten
cap	k ap	who is + ing or who will
clue	klou	nail
cow	ka w	your case
key	ki	who, what, that
lap	l ap	he/she/it is + ing or will
lee	li	he/she/it or to read
lisa	li sa	read this
map	m ap	i am + ing or i will
nap	n ap	we will or we will
poo	pou	for
sack	sa k	who is, what is
sack app	sa k ap	what is + ing
sync	senk	five
set	sèt	seven
see	si	if, sure, saw
seal	si l	if he/she/it

seem	si m	if i
sin	si n	if we
sis (sister)	sis	six
sue	sou	on
van cat	venn kat	twenty-four
van sync	venn senk	twenty-five
van sis	venn sis	twenty-six
van set	venn sèt	twenty-seven
wall	wòl	role
well	wè l	see it

👁 Tip

The space does not alter the pronunciation in *Ba W, Ka W, Sa W di, M ap,* and *L ap*. The single-letter words blend in with the words that precede or follow; they sound like *bow, cow, Saudi, map,* and *lap*.

Using the above set of words, we can make up the sentences below. Note that the word *met* is to be pronounced in Creole as *[meyt]*.

English	Kreyòl
They jinxed her	Yo met bouch sou li
She'll give you the cards	L ap ba W kat yo
She's the one who'll give you the cards	Li k ap ba W kat yo
She'll tell me if she sees them	L ap di M si L wè yo
I am learning Creole	M ap aprann Kreyòl
I already know how to speak Creole	Mwen konn pale Kreyòl deja
What's happening?	Sa k ap fèt?
Who told you that?	Ki è ski di W sa?
What role does she play?	Ki wol li jwe?
If she knew, she wouldn't do it	Si L te konnen, li pa t ap fè L
They didn't see it	Yo pa t wè L

11- Verb Conjugation

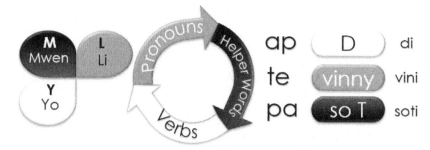

When conjugating verbs in Creole, the verb remains constant, regardless of the tense or pronoun. Instead of modifying the verb itself, some helper words are used in all cases to establish the proper mood or tense. Some verbs are considered helper words because they are sometimes followed by another verb. The most common helper words are:

Helper Words Including Negative Sentences			
ap *[ahp]*	Ing form, will	**pap** *[pah]*	won't, not + ing
pa *[pah]*	not	**pa t** *[paht]*	didn't
te *[tey]*	past tense	**t ap** *[tahp]*	would
ta *[tah]*	would	**pa t ap** *[pah-tahp]*	wouldn't
ka *[kah]*	can	**ta ka** *[tah-kah]*	could have
te ka *[tey-kah]*	could	**pa t ka** *[paht-kah]*	couldn't
pwal *[pwahl]*	will, is going to	**pa pwal** *[pah-pwahl]*	not going to
te pwal *[tey-pwahl]*	was going to	**ta pwal** *[tah-pwahl]*	was going to
konn *[kon]*	to know	**dwe** *[du-ey]*	must
fò *[fo]*	must	**vle** *[vley]*	to want

Let's revisit the old: **li vini chak Samdi** sentence from earlier and replace **Samdi** with the other days of the week, and the months and other time related expressions like tomorrow, yesterday, last month, next year, etc. My hope is that you've started to develop the confidence to practice out loud, engage in conversations, and begin impressing your friends, colleagues or loved ones. With this larger set of modal helper words, we can continue exploring some additional tenses.

Present Tense

Kreyòl	English
Mwen pale	I Speak
Ou pale	You Speak
Li pale	He/She speaks
Nou pale	We Speak
Nou pale	You Speak
Yo pale	They Speak

The abbreviated form of the pronouns is used when the verb begins with a vowel, except in the case of the first singular person where the full and abbreviated forms are used interchangeably.

Kreyòl	English
M sòti	I go out
Ou sòti	You go out
Li sòti	He/She goes out
Nou sòti	We go out
Nou sòti	You go out
Yo sòti	They go out

Past Tense

Kreyòl	English
Mwen te ale	I went
Ou te ale	You went
Li te ale	He/She went
Nou te ale	We went
Nou te ale	You went
Yo te ale	They went

Progressive Negative Form

Kreyòl	English
Mwen pap manje	I'm not eating
Ou pap manje	You aren't eating
Li pap manje	He/She isn't eating
Nou pap manje	We aren't eating
Nou pap manje	You aren't eating
Yo pap manje	They aren't eating

Using *Can*

Kreyòl	English
Mwen ka fè L	I can do it
Ou ka fè L	You can do it
Li ka fè L	He/She can do it
Nou ka fè L	We can do it
Nou ka fè L	You can do it
Yo ka fè L	They can do it

Past Tense of *vini*

Kreyòl	English
Mwen te vini	I came
Ou te vini	You came
Li te vini	He, she, it came
Nou te vini	We came
Nou te vini	You came
Yo te vini	They came

Negative

Kreyòl	English
Mwen pa vini	I don't come
Ou pa vini	You don't come
Li pa vini	He, she, it doesn't come

Nou pa vini	We don't come
Nou pa vini	You don't come
Yo pa vini	They don't come

Progressive Negative – *pap* is a combination of *pa* & *ap*

Kreyòl	English
Mwen pap vini	I'm not coming
Ou pap vini	You aren't coming
Li pap vini	He, she, it isn't coming
Nou pap vini	We aren't coming
Nou pap vini	You aren't coming
Yo pap vini	They aren't coming

Past Negative – *pa t* is a combination of *pa* & *te*, with te abbreviated as *t*

Kreyòl	English
Mwen pa t vini	I didn't come
Ou pa t vini	You didn't come
Li pa t vini	He, she, it didn't come
Nou pa t vini	We didn't come
Nou pa t vini	You didn't come
Yo pa t vini	They didn't come

Past Progressive

Kreyòl	English
Mwen t ap tann ni	I was waiting for her / him
Ou t ap tann yo?	Were you waiting for them?
Li t ap tann mwen	She was waiting for me
Nou t ap tann ni	We were waiting for her / him
Nou t ap tann mwen	Were you waiting for me?
Yo t ap tann nou	They were waiting for us

Negative & future tense, pap is a combination of pa & ap

Kreyòl	English
Mwen pap ka eksplike W	I won't be able to explain it to you
Ou pap ka eksplike M	You won't be able to explain it to me
Li pap ka eksplike yo	He won't be able to explain it to them
Nou pap ka eksplike L	You won't be able to explain it to her / him
Yo pap ka eksplike nou	They won't be able to explain it to us

Days of the Week

Let's replace **Samdi** with the other days of the week. Note that, whereas in English all the names of the days of the week end with **day**, in Kreyòl most end with **di**. The only exception is Dimanch, which begins instead of ending with **di**.

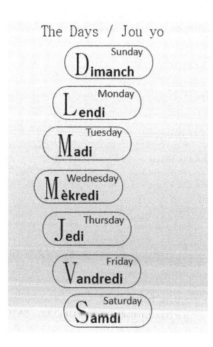

The Days / Jou yo

English	Kreyòl
Sunday	**Dimanch**
Monday	**Lendi**
Tuesday	**Madi**
Wednesday	**Mèkredi**
Thursday	**Jedi**
Friday	**Vandredi**
Saturday	**Samdi**

Sentences with the days of the week

English	Kreyòl
I'm coming on Sunday	M ap vini Dimanch
You're coming on Monday	W ap vini Lendi
He's coming on Tuesday	L ap vini Madi
We're coming on Wednesday	N ap vini Mèkredi
You're coming on Thursday	N ap vini Jedi
They're coming on Friday	Y ap vini Vandredi
They're coming on Saturday	Y ap vini Samdi

Sentences with vin, the abbreviated form of vini

English	Kreyòl
I'm supposed to come see you in January	Mwen sipoze vin wè W an Janvye
You're supposed to come see us in February	Ou sipoze vin wè N an Fevriye
She's supposed to come see them in March	Li sipoze vin wè yo an Mas
We're supposed to come see her in April	Nou sipoze vin wè L an Avril
You're supposed to come see me in May	Nou sipoze vin wè M an Me
They're supposed to come see him in June	Yo sipoze vin wè L an Jen

The Months

English	Kreyòl	English	Kreyòl
January	Janvye	July	Jiyè
February	Fevriye	August	Out
March	Mas	September	Septanm
April	Avril	October	Oktòb
May	Me	November	Novanm
June	Jen	December	Desanm

The Months/Mwa yo

Janvye / January	**J**iyè / July
Fevriye / February	**O**ut / August
Mas / March	**S**eptanm / September
Avril / April	**O**ktòb / October
Me / May	**N**ovanm / November
Jen / June	**D**esanm / December

Sentences with the Months

English	Kreyòl
I came in January	Mwen te vini an Janvye
You came in February	Ou te vini an Fevriye
She came in March	Li te vini an Mas
We came in April	Nou te vini an Avril
You came in May	Nou te vini an Me
They came in June	Yo te vini an Jen

More Sentences with the Months

English	Kreyòl
I came in July	Mwen te vini an Jiyè
You came in August	Ou te vini an Out
He came in September	Li te vini an Septanm
We came in October	Nou te vini an Oktòb
You came in November	Nou te vini an Novanm
They came in December	Yo te vini an Desanm

The subtle difference between **mèt** and **ka** – **Mèt** is used for happenings in the future or when you want to take or give permission to do something.

English	Kreyòl
I can come in January	Mwen mèt vini an Janvye
You can come in February	Ou mèt vini an Fevriye
He can come in March	Li mèt vini an Mas
We can come in April	Nou mèt vini an Avril
You can come in May	Nou mèt vini an Me
We can come in June	Yo mèt vini an Jen

Ka is used when someone has the ability to do something, or when you are allowed to do something to discuss possibility in the future.

English	Kreyòl
I may come in July	Mwen ka vini an Jiyè
You may come in August	Ou ka vini an Out
He may come in September	Li ka vini an Septanm
We may come in October	Nou ka vini an Oktòb
You may come in November	Nou ka vini an Novanm
We may come in December	Yo ka vini an Desanm

I'm sure there'll be a time when you'll have to set some expectations or tell a story during which you'll need to specify whether something happened in the past or will happen in the future. You may have to talk about what's happening to you today or what you plan to do in the future. To facilitate those types of conversations, you need to know words like: now, yesterday, today, tomorrow, and others.

English	Kreyòl
the other day	lòtre jou
day before yesterday	avan yè
yesterday	yè
today	jodi a
now	kounyè a
tomorrow	demen
day after tomorrow	apre demen
in a few days	nan kèlke jou

Let's now use the word **vini** with the above time related expressions to ask questions. There're two basic ways to ask questions; they either begin with the pronoun or with the very common combination **ès ke** pronounced [S K]. You can pretty much repeat everyone of the following questions by adding ès ke before the pronoun.

English	Kreyòl
Are you coming now?	W ap vini kounyè a?
Are you all coming today?	N ap vini jodi a?
Did you all come yesterday?	Nou te vini yè?
Are they coming tomorrow?	Y ap vini demen?
Are you coming later?	W ap vini pi ta?
Did they come the other day?	Yo te vini lòtre jou?

Except for the question mark at the end, there's basically no difference in structure between the question and the answer. The only difference is in the tone.

English	Kreyòl
I'm coming now	M ap vini kounyè a
We are coming today	N ap vini jodi a
We came yesterday	Nou te vini yè
They'll come tomorrow	Y ap vini demen
I'll come later	M ap vini pi ta

Now let's put to use the following words: **ankò, deja, janm, san, toujou**. **Ankò** is used for both *"again"* and *"anymore"* or *"no more."* It translates to *"again"* when it's an affirmative sentence and to *"no more"* when **pa** is introduced to transform the sentence into a negative one. **Ankò** is another widely-used word that's connected to English via French. I'm sure you've, at some point, gone to a play or the opera and have cheered "Encore, Encore" as a way to request that a particular segment of the show be repeated. Both **janm** and **jamè** mean never; the latter is closer to French and is rarely used.

English	Kreyòl
again, anymore, no more	ankò *[ahN-ko]*
already	deja *[dey-zhah]*
always	toujou *[too-zhoo]*

76

never	janm, jamè *[zhah-me]*
rapid, quick, quickly	rapid, vit *[rah-peed]*
slow, slowly	dousman *[doos-mahN]*
with	a, ak, avè, avèk
without	san

It's sometimes more appropriate to use the abbreviated form of verbs such as **vini** as you will see in the examples below. Typically, when the verb is the last word of the sentence, it's best to use the full form. However, when another word follows the verb, although it isn't absolutely necessary, it's preferable that you use the abbreviated form **vin**. **Fini**, which means *"to finish,"* follows the exact same principle where it's more appropriate to use the abbreviated form **fin** when the verb isn't the last word in the sentence.

English	Kreyòl
I'm coming back	M ap vin ankò or M ap retounen
We aren't coming anymore	Nou pap vin ankò
I'm still coming	M ap toujou vini
Aren't you coming anymore?	Ou pap vin ankò?
Are you coming with her?	W ap vin avè L?
She isn't coming with us	Li pap vini avè N
Can you come with me?	Ou ka vin avè M?
Yes, I'm coming with you	Wi, M ap vin avè W
I'm not coming with them	Mwen pap vin avèk yo
She's never coming	Li pap janm vini
She's never coming back	Li pap janm vini ankò or li pap janm retounen
We're coming without them	N ap vini san yo
They always come	Yo toujou vini
He always comes with them	Li toujou vin avèk yo
He never comes without them	Li pa janm vin san yo
Repeat it slowly so I can understand	Repete L dousman pou M ka konprann

While in English most of the interrogative pronouns begin with **wh**, their Kreyòl equivalents begin with **ki**.

Interrogative Pronouns

English	Kreyòl
who	ki ès, ki moun
what	ki sa
when	ki lè
where	ki bò, ki kote
why	pou ki
how	ki jan, kòman, kouman
how much	konbyen

While verbs vary very little in English, in Kreyòl, they don't vary at all. They remain constant regardless of the subject or tense. The helper words are used to mark the tense. Here are some additional common verbs to experiment with.

Common Verbs

English	Kreyòl
to announce	anonse [ah-nohN-sey]
to arrive	rive [ree-vey]
to be named, call, yell	rele [rey-ley]
to begin	kòmanse [ko-mahN-sey]
to believe	kwè [kwe]
to bleed	blese [bley-sey]
to bring, carry	pote [poh-tey]
to bring along	mennen [mehN-nehN]

to buy	achte *[ahsh-tey]*
to close	fèmen*[fe-mehN]*
to come back	tounen, retounen *[rey-too-nehN]*
to criticize	kritike *[kree-tee-key]*
to do, to make	fè *[fe]*
to drink	bwè *[bwe]*
to eat, food	manje *[mahN-zhey]*
to enter	antre, rantre *[rahN-trey]*
to find	jwenn *[zhwen]*
to finish	fin, fini *[fee-nee]*
to forget	bliye *[blee-ee-ey]*
to go out	soti, sòti *[so-tee]*
to heal	geri *[mehN-n]*
to hide	kache *[kah-shey]*
to know	konn, konnen *[kohN-nehN]*
to learn	aprann *[ah-prahn]*
to leave	pati *[pah-tee]*
to be released from	lage *[lah-gey]*
to look like, resemble	sanble *[sahN-bley]*
to love, like	renmen *[rehN-mehN]*
to meet	rankontre *[rahN-kohN-trey]*
to pass	pase *[pah-sey]*
to prefer	prefere *[prey-fey-rey]*
to pull	rale *[rah-ley]*
to read	li *[lee]*
to refuse	refize *[rey-fee-zey]*
to remember	sonje *[sohN-zhey]*
to say, tell	di *[dee]*
to see	wè *[we]*
to sign	siyen *[see-ee-ehN]*
to speak	pale *[pah-ley]*
to split	krache *[krah-shey]*
to start over	rekòmanse *[rey-ko-mahN-sey]*

to stay	ret, rete [rey-tey]
to support	sipòte [see-po-tey]
to travel	vwayaje [vwah-ee-ah-zhey]
to try	eseye [ey-sey-ee-ey]
to understand	konprann [kohN-prahn]
to wait	tan [trahn]
to wake up	reveye [rey-vey-yey]
to want	vle [vley]
to warm up	chofe [show-fey]
to write	ekri [ey-kree]

Manje is both a verb and a noun; it means both "food" and "to eat." As a result, it's not rare to see it used twice in a sentence. For example:

I ate all my food	**Mwen manje tout manje M nan**
I haven't eaten my food yet	**Mwen poko manje manje M nan**
She's done eating her food	**Li fin manje tout manje L la**
She didn't eat her meal	**Se pa manje pa L la li manje**
She ate my meal	**Se manje pa M nan li manje**

It's not uncommon to have sentences without verbs. In the majority of cases, it's the verb "*to be*" that's omitted in the sentence.

English	Kreyòl
How old are you?	Ki laj ou?
I'm well	Mwen byen
I'm well, I'm in good form	Mwen an fòm
You're quick	Ou rapid
Are you the fastest?	Ou pi rapid?
You're faster than I	Ou pi rapid pase M
They're happy	Yo kontan
They're hungry	Yo grangou
I'm full	Vant mwen plen
She's thirsty	Li swaf
We're tired	Nou fatige

The adjectives can either follow or precede the nouns. Similar to English, when two or more adjectives are used to describe the nouns, each adjective is separated by a comma and the last one on the list is typically preceded by the single-letter word *e* or *epi*, followed by the corresponding pronoun. To describe a beautiful house, the sentences have pretty much the same structure in both languages, except in the last two egzanp where **e** or **epi** is used along with the pronoun right before the last adjective.

What a beautiful house	**A la on bèl kay**
This is a beautiful house	**Sa a se on bèl kay**
That house is big and beautiful	**Kay sa a gwo epi li bèl**
That house is big, beautiful, and expensive	**Kay sa a gow, li bèl, e li chè**

Let's introduce some basic adjectives to apply to the verb list shown earlier.

When I'm not focused on writing Kreyòl books to help you speak the language, I work in the IT industry as a Project Manager. For the past twenty-one years, I've been working for Japanese companies. My current employer is the fourth Japanese company I've worked with directly. In Japanese culture, they don't like to use the words *bad* or *fail*. They use *no good* instead. We do something similar in Kreyòl. The direct translation for the word *bad* which is **move**, is almost never used in this sense. We exclusively use *not good* instead, which translates to **pa bon**.

English	Kreyòl
angry	move *[moh-vey]*
bad	pa bon *[pah-bohN]*
cold	frèt *[freht]*
good	bon *[bohN]*
hot	cho *[shoh]*
ready	pare *[pah-rey]*
salty	sale *[sah-ley]*
spicy, hot	pike *[pee-key]*
tasty	gou *[goo]*

We can now qualify (**kalifye**) the food using the adjectives (**adjektif**) we just learned. Note that in those examples, **manje** is used as a noun and as we saw before in the majority (**majorite**) of those cases (**ka**), the verb (**vèb**) *"to be"* is left out of these sentences.

English	Kreyòl
The food is very good	Manje a bon anpil
The food is very tasty	Manje a gou anpil
The food is spicy	Manje a pike
The food is ready	Manje a pare
The food is hot	Manje a cho
The food is cold	Manje a frèt
The food is very spicy	Manje a pike anpil
The food isn't spicy	Manje a pa pike
The food isn't cooked yet	Manje a poko kuit
The food isn't ready yet	Manje a poko pare
That's too much food	Manje a twòp
That's too much food for me	Manje sa a twòp pou mwen
That's just enough food for me	Manje sa a kont mwen
You gave me too much food	Ou ban M twòp manje
Why did you give me so much food?	Pou kisa ou ban M tout manje sa a?
Where's the food	Kot manje a?
What are you going to do with all this food?	Sa N ap fè a tout manje sa a?
They'd rather leave their food for later	Yo pito kite manje yo a pou pi ta
I don't have any money to buy food	Mwen pa gen lajan pou M achte manje
They don't like spicy food	Yo pa renmen manje pike
Haitians love food that's very spicy	Ayisyen renmen manje ki pike anpil
The foreigners don't like spicy food	Etranje yo pa renmen manje pike
Why is the food so spicy	Pou kisa manje a pike konsa?
The food isn't really spicy	Manje a pa pyès pike
It isn't true that the food is spicy	Se pa vre ke manje a pike

In most of the sentences below, *manje* is used as a verb, and in certain cases, it's used as both the verb and noun.

English	Kreyòl
I don't want to eat yet	Mwen poko vle manje
I'm not eating yet	Mwen pap manje kounyè a
The kids don't want to eat	Ti moun yo pa vle manje

They've finished eating all the food	Yo fin manje tout manje a
Your mom just got done eating	Manman W fèk fin manje
Who cooked the food?	Ki moun ki fè manje a?
Who'is cooking the food?	Ki moun k ap kuit manje a?
Why don't they eat?	Pou kisa yo pa manje?
Because they aren't hungry	Paske yo pa grangou
They'll eat later	Y ap manje pi ta
Why don't you want to eat?	Pou kisa ou pa vle manje?
At what time should I come eat?	A ki lè pou M vin manje
How many times a day do you eat?	Konbyen fwa pa jou ou manje?
I don't want anymore	Mwen pa vle ankò
I'm full	Vant mwen plen
What are you drinking?	Kisa W ap bwè?
I'm almost done eating	Mwen prèske fin manje
She ate everything	Li manje tout
They just finished eating	Yo fèk fin manje
They'll eat later	Y ap manje pi ta
They'll eat when they're hungry	Y ap maje lè yo grangou
They ate it all (everything)	Yo manje tout manje a nèt
They went to eat at the restaurant	Yo t al manje nan restoran
They just came from the restaurant	Yo fèk sot nan restoran
They didn't eat because they weren't hungry	Yo pa t manje paske yo potko grangou

Konvèsasyon

This is a konvèsasyon between someone who cooked for their significant other, who's grateful and raving about how tasty the food is. From this konvèsasyon, you'll see how words and expressions like yesterday, hungry, love, since, now, honey, to know, wash, always, and a few others are used.

English	Kreyòl
Have you eaten yet?	Ou manje deja?
No, I haven't	Non, Mwen poko manje
Do you want to eat now?	Ès ke ou vle manje kounyè a?
Yes, I'm very hungry	Wi, M grangou anpil
I haven't eaten since yesterday	Mwen pa manje depi yè
Go wash your hands	Al lave men W
I'll warm up the food for you	M ap chofe manje a pou ou
The food is very tasty	Manje a bon anpil
I made it with love	Mwen fè L avèk lanmou
You should eat it all	Fò W manje tout wi
You know I always eat all my food	Ou konnen M toujou manje tout manje M
I know that	M konn sa
Thank you darling	Mèsi cheri

Anndan is probably going to be a hard one to pronounce. Note the double *n* in the first syllable; which means that the *n* isn't silent. However, in the second syllable, it's a regular nasal sound, and the *n* is silent and pronounced as *an* in avantgarde.

English	Kreyòl
against, enough, tale, account	kont *[kohNt]*
all	tout *[toot]*
alone	pou kont + pronoun i.e. pou kont mwen
everybody	tout moun *[toot-moon]*
everything	tout bagay *[toot-bah-gah y]*
inside	anndan an *[ahN-dahN-ahN]*
just	fèk *[fek]*
like	kon *[kohN]*
nobody	pyès moun *[pee-es-moon]*
nothing	anyen, pyès bagay *[ahN-yehN]*
only	sèlman *[sel-mahN]*
outside	deyò a *[dey-yo-ah]*
together	ansanm *[ahN-sahNm]*

English can be confusing even for native speakers when it comes to which preposition (**prepozisyon**) to use between *"in"* and *"on"* to describe (**dekri**) whether you are in a car or on a plane. The preposition *"at"* is also used extensively in English. In Kreyòl, we either use no preposition at all or we use *nan*, which translates to *"in."*

English	Kreyòl
We're out	Nou deyò
We're outside	Nou deyò a
We're inside	Nou anndan
We're inside	Nou anndan an
We're home	Nou lakay
We're at home	Nou lakay la
We're at church	Nou legliz
We're at the church	Nou nan legliz la
We're at school	Nou lekòl
We're at the school	Nou nan lekòl la

We're at the hospital	Nou lopital
We're at the hospital	Nou nan lopital la
We're in the car	Nou nan machin nan
We're on the way	Nou nan wout
We just arrived	Nou fèk rive
We're on the airplane	Nou nan avyon an
We're all here	Nou tout la
We all came together	Nou tout vini ansanm
We brought everything	Nou pote tout bagay

Below are some example sentences where words like **sèlman, ansanm, apre, menm lè,** and **avan** are used.

English	Kreyòl
Are you all coming?	Ès ke nou tout ap vini?
No, I'm coming alone	Non, M ap vini pou kò M
No, I'm the only one who's coming	Non, mwen menm sèlman k ap vini
No, only Mark is coming	Non, Mark sèlman k ap vini
Yes, we're all coming together	Wi, nou tout ap vini ansanm
We'll get there before you	N ap rive anvan W
Everybody's coming	Tout moun ap vini
They got there a little bit after you	Yo rive on ti moman apre W
I suspect we'll get there at the same time	M sispèk N ap rive an menm tan
I suspect we'll get there at the same time	M sispèk N ap rive a menm lè
He went to church	L al legliz
He went to the school	L al lekòl la
He went to the hospital	L al lopital la
He went to the dentist	L ale kay dantis
He went to see his dentist	L al wè dantis li
He went to see his doctor	L al wè doktè L

Konvèsasyon

Below is a short konvèsasyon using words that were recently introduced.

Where are you?	Kote nou?
We're on the way	Nou sou wout
How about you?	E ou menm?
I'm already there	Mwen rive deja
You're quick my friend	Ou rapid papa*
You know it	Ou konnen
I'm almost there	M prèske rive
Will you be happy to see me?	W ap kontan wè M?
Of course	Nòmalman

*papa is father or Dad; however, it's sometimes commonly used as my friend. Similarly manman, which normally means mother is used in the same way for a female friend.

Here are some practical sentences using the common verbs, adverbs, and the timeframes we saw earlier.

English	Kreyòl
What's your name?	Kòman ou rele?
My name is ...	Mwen rele ...
How are you?	Kòman W ye?
What's up?	Sa k pase?
What's wrong with you?	Sa W genyen? or ki sa W genyen?
I'm well	Mwen an fòm
I feel better today	M santi M pi byen jodi a
I don't feel well	M pa santi M byen
I have a headache	Tèt mwen fè M mal
I have a toothache	Dan M fè M mal
I have a tummy ache	Vant mwen fè M mal
Now I feel good	Kounyè a M santi M byen
Is this for me?	Sa a se pou mwen?
Yes, it's for you	Wi, se pou ou
I'm five years old	Mwen gen senk an
Today is colder than yesterday	Jodi a li fè pi frèt pase ye
Today is colder than all the other days	Jodi a li fè pi frèt pase tout jou yo
Today is the hottest day of the week	Jodi a se jou ki pi cho nan semèn nan
We're running late	N ap rive an reta
The plane is on time	Avyon an a lè
The bus is running late	Bis la an reta
We're almost there	Nou prèske rive
She's going out later	L ap soti pi ta
They don't want to work on Sundays	Yo pa vle travay le Dimanch
They can walk	Yo ka mache
They're playing outside	Y ap jwe deyò a
She doesn't want to eat now	Li pa vle manje kounyè a
Wait for us if you get there before us	Ret tann nou si W rive anvan
I'm the only one who's coming	Mwen menm sèlman k ap vini
We're all going together	Nou tout ap ale ansanm

Pray for the country	Priye pou peyi a
Pray for the kids	Priye pou ti moun yo
Always pray for the kids	Toujou priye pou pitit ou yo
Never stop praying for your kids	Pa janm sispann priye pou pitit ou yo
Ask God for forgiveness	Mande Bon Dye padon
She screams louder than anyone	Li rele'pi fò pase tout moun

The word **fèt** has several meanings; it's sometimes a noun and means *"party"* or *"birthday."* It also translates to two different verbs *"to be born"* or *"must."* In the latter case, it's always followed by pou, which literally (**literalman**) means *"for."*

There are several ways of translating "must": **dwe, fèt,** or **fò**. Just like in English **dwe** is immediately followed by a verb, but **fèt** and **fò** are used in a special manner where the former is followed by **pou**, and then the verb and in the latter case, the pronoun follows **fò**, which is in turn, is followed by the verb. Pa egzanp:

She must eat	**Fò L manje**
You must ask for forgiveness	**Ou dwe mande padon**
I must go now	**Fò M ale kounyè a**
They must visit their dad	**Yo fèt pou yo vizite papa yo**
She must train every morning	**Fò L antrene chak maten**

The following table contains some expressions or verbs that are usually followed by another verb or a pronoun. Make sure you can recognize (**rekonèt**) them, as they will mostly come up in konvèsasyon with native speakers.

English	Kreyòl
must, to owe	dwe
must	Fò followed by pronoun
must	fèt followed by pou then pronoun
must not	pa dwe
must not	pa fèt followed by pou then pronoun
should have	ta dwe
shouldn't have	pa ta dwe

party, to be born, must	fèt
must not	pa fèt
should have	ta fèt
shouldn't have	pa ta fèt
to be supposed to	sipoze
was supposed to	te sipoze, ta sipoze
to want	vle
to finish	fin or fini

"*To give*" is the only verb in Kreyòl that varies (**varye**), not because of the tenses nor the subject (**sijè**) but rather, it varies depending on (**depann de**) the objective personal (**pèsonèl**) pronoun that follows. "*To give*" can take one of three forms (**fòm**): **ba, ban,** or **bay**.

Who gave her the book?	**Ki ès ki ba L liv la?**
Who gave it to you?	**Ki ès ki ba ou L?**
I gave them all the money	**Mwen ba yo tout kòb la**
I gave them this Creole book	**Mwen ba yo liv Kreyòl sa a**
A friend gave it to me	**Se on zanmi ki ban mwen L**
He gives us many problems	**Li ba nou anpil pwoblèm**
He gives us many problems	**Li ban N anpil pwoblèm**
You're causing trouble	**W ap bay pwoblèm**
The boxer gave up on the fight	**Boksè a bay le gen**
Who's giving blood	**Ki ès k ap bay san**
I'm not giving any blood	**M pap bay pyès san**
I just gave blood	**M fèk bay san**
I volunteered to give blood	**Mwen volontè pou M bay san**

There are lots of homonyms in Creole, which can be confusing at first. Not to worry though, with practice you'll be able to figure out what's being said, and also pick the correct word to match the context. **Ba, ban** and **bay** have another meaning, which is "*let*." You can use the following rule to differentiate the two different meanings. If you're talking about a physical object it's "*to give,*" and it's "*let*" if it's not physical (**fizik**). **Kite** that we saw earlier is another translation for "*let*" and can be used in all the below cases. Here are some *egzanp* where the meaning is "*let*."

Let me go	**Ban M pase**
Let them see what you're doing	**Ba yo wè sa W ap fè**
Let me drive	**Ban M kondi**
Let me drive the car	**Ban M kondi machin nan**
Let me drive for you	**Ban M kondi pou ou**
Let me show you	**Ban M montre W**
Let her play with the doll	**Ba L jwe avèk poupe a**
She doesn't like to let him go out	**Li pa renmen kite L soti**
She doesn't let anyone come over	**Li pa kite pyès moun vin lakay li**
She didn't let them leave early	**Li pa t kite yo ale bonè**

The following table (**tab**) contains some additional common verbs. Match them with the nouns, adjectives, and pronouns that are also listed below to make up your own sentences. Imagine something you would like to say, find the Creole equivalent of the words that make up the sentences and string them together. The first few attempts may not work perfectly, but with practice you'll get there. Keep in mind though, that my blog is only a click away; bookmark it, pose a question (**kesyon**), start a konvèsasyon, inbox me; I'm happy to help you with any challenges you face.

English	Kreyòl
to adopte	adopte *[ah-dohp-tey]*
to ask	mande *[mahN-dey]*
to be	ès, se, ye *[es]*
to begin, start	kòmanse *[ko-mahN-sey]*
to believe	kwè *[kwe]*
to break	kraze *[ah-dohp-tey]*
to call, scream, yell	rele *[rey-ley]*
to carry	pote *[poh-tey]*
to close	fèmen *[fe-mehN]*
to continue	kontinye *[kohN-tee-nee-ey]*
to cook	kuit *[kweet]*
to create	kreye *[krey-ee-ey]*
to cry	kriye *[kree-ee-ey]*
to decide	deside *[dey-see-dey]*

91

to drive	kondi *[kohN-dee]*
to dry up	seche *[sah-shey]*
to explain	eksplike *[ehx-plee-key]*
to feel, smell	santi *[sahN-tee]*
to find	jwenn, twouve *[jwen]*
to fix	ranje *[rahN-zhey]*
to get up	leve *[ley-vey]*
to go down	desann *[dey-sahn]*
to go out	sot, soti, sòti *[soht]*
to go up	monte *[mohN-tey]*
to have to	oblije *[oh-blee-zhey]*
to hear	tande *[tahN-dey]*
to laugh	ri *[ree]*
to lay down	kouche *[koo-shey]*
to lean	apiye *[ah-pee-ee-ey]*
to learn	aprann *[ah-prahn]*
to leave	kite, pati *[kee-tey]*
to listen	koute *[koo-tey]*
to lose	pèdi *[pe-dee]*
to love, like	renmen *[rehN-mehN]*
to meet	rankontre *[rahN-kohN-trey]*
to open	ouvè *[oo-ve]*
to play	jwe *[zhwey]*
to pray	priye *[pree-ee-ey]*
to protect	pwoteje *[pwoh-tey-zhey]*
to put, wear	met, mete *[meht]*
to respect	respekte *[reys-peyk-tey]*
to run	kouri *[koo-ree]*
to show, teach	montre *[mohN-trey]*
to sit down	chita *[shee-tah]*
to sleep	dòmi *[do-mee]*
to smile	souri *[soo-ree]*
to stand up	kanpe *[kahN-pey]*

to stop	ret, rete, sispann *[reyt]*
to suffer	soufri *[soo-free]*
to support	sipòte *[see-po-tey]*
to take	pran *[prahN]*
to tare	chire *[shee-rey]*
to tell	rakonte *[rah-kohN-tey]*
to think	panse *[pahN-sey]*
to think, to reflect	reflechi *[rey-fley-shee]*
to understand	konprann *[kohN-prahn]*
to wait	tan *[tahN]*
to wake up	reveye *[rey-vey-ee-ey]*
to walk	mache *[mah-shey]*
to wash	lave *[lah-vey]*

Depending on the reason you're learning Kreyòl, I'm pretty sure that you'll need to use some or all of the following nouns, **lopital, legliz, lekòl, avyon, frè, sè, klinik, peyi, doktè, dantis**.

English	Kreyòl
adoption	adopsyon *[ah-dohp-see-ohN]*
airplane	avyon *[ah-vee-ohN]*
at the house	lakay la *[lah-kahy-lah]*
at the house	nan kay la *[nahN-kahy-lah]*
baby bottle	bibon *[bee-bohN]*
bottle	boutèy *[boo-te-y]*
brother	frè *[fre]*
can	mamit *[mah-meet]*
car	machin *[mah-sheen]*
chance	chans *[chahNs]*
church	legliz *[ley-gleez]*
clinic	klinik *[klee-neek]*
country	peyi *[pey-ee-ey]*
dentist	dantis *[dahN-tees]*
doctor	doktè *[dohk-te]*
family	fanmi *[fahN-mee]*

father	papa *[pah-pah]*
habit	abitid *[ah-bee-teed]*
half	mwatye *[mwah-tee-ey]*
hand	men *[mehN]*
history	istwa *[ees-twah]*
hospital	lopital *[loh-pee-tah l]*
house	kay *[kah y]*
kid	ti moun *[tee-moon]*
manner	jan *[jahN]*
message	mesaj *[mey-sahzh]*
middle	mitan *[mee-tahN]*
mother	manman *[mahN-mahN]*
my child	pitit mwen *[pee-teet-mwehN]*
need	anvi, bezwen *[ahN-vee]*
office	biwo *[bee-woh]*
pardon, to forgive	padon *[pah-dohN]*
people	moun *[moon]*
prayer	priyè *[pree-ee-e]*
rout	wout *[woot]*
school	lekòl *[ley-kol]*
sister	sè *[se]*
situation	sitiyasyon *[see-tee-ee-ah-see-ohN]*
surprise	sipriz *[see-preez]*
telephone	telefòn *[tey-ley-fo-n]*
thing	bagay *[bah-gah y]*
ticket	tikè *[tee-ke]*
wound	blesi *[bley-see]*

This resource isn't intended to be a dictionary (**diksyonè**). However, within these pages (**paj**), you'll discover (**dekouvri**) most of the words needed to say just about anything. As much as I can, I've been adding the cognates in parentheses (**parantèz**) to help you build your vocabulary. You should make a note (**nòt**) of the words you weren't already familiar with. In addition, as a fun

94

exercise (**egzèsis**), if I don't note the cognates, as I'm doing in this paragraph (**paragraph**), you should note the ones you personally (**pèsonèlman**) spot.

English	Kreyòl
during the night	nan nuit la
however, but	men
in a little while	touta lè
in a week	nan on semèn
in two days	nan de jou
in three months	nan twa mwa
in four years	nan kat ane
more	aprè midi a
next month	lòt mwa a
next week	lòt semèn
next year	lòt ane
on time	a lè
this morning	maten an
time, when	lè
tonight	a swè a

If you're a medical professional, your patients won't worry about the fact that you may or may not know their language. They'll most likely engage you in konvèsasyon. If your interpreter isn't in the room or if you're already reading this resource and are starting to get familiar with the language, you may hear some of the phrases that follow.

English	Kreyòl
How are you doctor?	Kòman W ye doktè?
Good morning doctor	Bon jou doktè
Good afternoon doctor	Bon swa doktè
See you tomorrow	Na wè demen
I'm not well at all	M pa bon menm
I don't feel well	M pa santi M byen
We're happy	Nou kontan
They aren't bad	Yo pa twò mal
It's too expensive	Sa a twò chè

He's sick	Li malad
I'm hot	Mwen cho
I'm not hot	Mwen pa cho
She's always cold	Li toujou frèt
The car broke down	Machin nan an pàn
My tummy's hurts	Vant mwen fè M mal
We're all tired	Nou tout fatige
He doesn't want to tell his mom how he feels	Li pa vle di manman L ki jan L santi L
They don't know why she's crying	Yo pa konn pou ki L ap kriye
We know where he is	Nou konn ki kote L ye
Hi mom is the one who decides	Se manman L ki deside
I'm sleepy	M anvi dòmi
She can't sleep	Li pa ka dòmi
I never sleep	M pa janm dòmi
I have a hart time sleeping	M gen pwoblèm pou M dòmi
They need some rest	Yo bezwen repo

If you're an adoptive parent or you work with kids at an orphanage or a church, you may hear or may have to use some of the sentences below.

English	Kreyòl
You can take all of it	Ou mèt pran tout
Can we go play?	Ès ke nou mèt al jwe?
You can play with them	Ou mèt jwe avèk yo
She doesn't want to play with me	Li pa vle jwe avè M
She took it without asking	Li pran L san L pa mande
Go wash your hands before you eat	Al lave men W anvan W manje
The Haiti fare is always high	Tikè Ayiti a toujou chè
Let me get in front of you	Ban M pase devan W
She loves all her kids	Li renmen tout pitit li yo
The sun is hot	Solèy la cho
The moon is bright	La lin nan klere
She doesn't respect anyone	Li pa respekte pyès moun
I can't understand what he says	Mwen pa ka konprann sa L di

She understands everything you say	Li konprann tout sa W di
We just started learning Creole	Nou fèk kòmanse aprann Kreyòl
We've become Creole experts	Nou fin konn pale Kreyòl net
I don't know how to speak Creole yet	Mwen pako konn pale Kreyòl
We're learning Creole	N ap aprann Kreyòl
The whole family is learning Creole	Tout fanmi an ap aprann Kreyòl
Wait for us at the school	Ret tann nou nan lekòl la
She's never going back to New York	Li pap janm retounen Nou Yòk

If you're at a restaurant or you're shopping, you may hear or may have to use some of the sentences below.

English	Kreyòl
The cola is cold	Kola a glase
The beer isn't cold	Byè a pa glase
The beer is colder	Byè a pi glase
The water isn't that cold	Dlo a pa pi glase pase sa
There's nothing left	Pa gen pyès ki rete
How much does it cost?	Konbyen li koute?
How much is that?	Sa fè konbyen?
How much for all of them?	Konbyen pou tout?

Konvèsasyon

The neighbor visits his friend who isn't at home. His son lets the friend know his dad is at church and takes him to the church to meet his dad.

Is your Dad there?	Papa W la?
No, he isn't	Non, li pa la
Where did he go?	Kote L ale?
He went to church	L al legliz
Has he been gone long?	Sa gen lontan depi L ale?
Yes, it's been a while	Wi, sa gen on bon ti moman
When is he coming back?	A ki lè L ap retounen?
I don't know	M pa konnen
Is the church far?	Ès ke legliz la lwen?
No, it's not far	Non, li pa lwen
Can you take me to the church?	Ou ka mennen M legliz la?
Yes, follow me	Wi, swiv mwen
Let's go	An N ale

12- Articles (Atik yo)

There are six definite (**definit**) articles: *a, an, le, la, lan, and nan*. Sometimes, two of them are used as opposed to just one. Sometimes they are also used along with a demonstrative or possessive pronoun. Egzanp:

English	Kreyòl
My Car	Machin mwen an
My Pants	Pantalon M nan
That Bank	Bank sa a
The Airplane	Avyon an
The Broom	Bale a
The Doctor	Doktè a
The Food	Manje a
The Key	Kle a
The Moon	La lin nan
The Office	Biwo a
The Old Men	Le pè a
Your House	Kay ou a

Notice in the last examples above a very common usage of article pairs or article plus pronoun that aren't used in English.

- *le* and *a*
- *la* and *nan*
- *sa* and *a,*
- *mwen* and *a*
- *ou* and *a*

Anvan means *"before."* An easy way to remember this word is to use the following memory aid: it's **V** is sandwiched between two sets of **an**.

Nan is one of the six definite articles, but it also means *"in."* You'll remember it by looking at it this way: it's **a** sandwiched between two **n**'s. These are additional examples to show you how I personally use R2R. Find your sweet spot to make it work for you.

13- Sentence Structure

Kreyòl sentence structure is very similar to English, with a few of minor differences:

1- As mentioned earlier it's quite common to have a Kreyòl sentence that lacks a verb. The verb "*to be*," which is very prevalent in English and not so much in Kreyòl, is often omitted. Egzanp:

   a. I'm satisfied = **mwen satisfè**
   b. they're in danger = **yo an danje**
   c. she isn't up to it = **li pa sou sa**

2- When using simple phrasing, the article succeeds the noun instead of preceding it. Sometimes, two articles are used in conjunction with one another. In other cases, a possessive pronoun (*mwen, ou, li, nou, yo*) and an article are used in conjunction.

   a. the bank = **bank la**
   b. the aspirin = **aspirin nan**
   c. the broom = **bale a**
   d. the old man = **le pè a**
   e. my food = **manje mwen an**
   f. your bread = **pen w nan**
   g. the students = **elèv yo**
   h. her kids = **pitit li yo**

When a complete Kreyòl sentence contains a verb, the resulting structure is very similar to English. The major difference is that the definite or indefinite article precedes the noun in English whereas in Creole it succeeds the noun.

English	Kreyòl
I just started learning Creole	M fèk kòmanse aprann Kreyòl
I already know how to speak Creole	Mwen konn pale Kreyòl deja
Who gave you the medication?	Ki ès ki ba W medikaman yo?
Your ear is infected	Zòrèy ou enfekte
You have an infection in your ear	Ou fè enfeksyon nan zòrèy
You have to go to therapy	Fò W al nan terapi a
You have to put in the effort	Fò W fè efò
She adopted a Haitian kid	Li adopte on ti moun Ayiti

They plan to adopt another kid	Yo gen plan pou Y adopte on lòt ti moun
He is leaving with me next week	L ap pati avè M lòt semèn
We don't know when we're coming back	Nou pa konn ki lè N ap tounen
We're traveling together	N ap vwayaje ansanm
Are you all coming back together?	Ès ke nou tout ap retounen menm lè?
You guys aren't coming anymore, are you?	Nou pap vin ankò?
They asked her how old she is	Yo mande L ki laj li genyen
They left without me	Y ale kite M
I told you this is my suitcase	Mwen di W se malèt pa M nan sa
This isn't my car	Se pa machin mwen an sa

14- Adverbs (Advèb)

An adverb often describes (**dekri**) how well a subject performs (**pèfòme**) a given action. Many adverbs are formed by adding –*ly* in English or –*man* [*mahN*] in Kreyòl to the adjective. However, some adverbs and adverbial expressions (**ekspresyon**) aren't formed from adjectives and don't end in –*man*. Those types are generally (*jeneralman*) short and, as such, relatively (*relativman*) easy to remember. Below are some of the most common adverbs in regards to place (**plas**). Remember to use R2R for memorization.

Adverbs	Advèb
above	an wo [ahN-woh]
after	aprè, apre [ah-prey]
a little bit	on ti jan [ohN-tee-zhahN]
before	avan, anvan [ahN-vahN]
behind, back side	dèyè [de-ye]
between	ant [ahNt]
close by	tou pre a [too-prey-ah]
far	lwen [lwehN]
in	an, nan [nahN]
in front	devan [dey-vahN]
left side	bò goch [bo-goh-sh]
near	pre [prey]
next to, on the side	sou kote, bò kote [bo-koh-tey]
normally	nòmalman [no-mahl-mahN]
on	sou [soo]
on top	an wo [ahN-woh]
practically	pratikman [prah-teek-mahN]
right side	bò dwat [bo-dwaht]
straight	dwat [dwaht]
technically	teknikman [teyk-neek-mahN]
to the left	a goch [ah-gohsh]
to the right	a dwat [ah-dwaht]
under	an ba [dwaht]
very far	byen lwen [bee-ehN-lwehN]
very near	byen pre [bee-ehN-prey]

where	ki bò *[kee-bo]*
where	ki kote *[kee-koh-tey]*
where	kote *[koh-tey]*

Sample Sentences

English	Kreyòl
Between these two, who is telling the truth?	Ant de moun sa yo ki ès k ap di verite?
Don't let me get in front of you	Piga ou kite M pran devan W
Don't look back	Pa gade dèyè
Don't put your foot in the water	Pa met pye W nan dlo a
I am leaving with my husband	M ap pati avèk mari M
I'll give you a shot in your arm	M ap ba W on piki nan bra
I'm going to the hospital right after	Mwen pwal nan lopital la apre sa
He's not leaving without his wife	Li pap pati san madanm ni
Look straight ahead	Gade dwat devan w
Remove your hand from my pocket	Retire men W nan pòch mwen
She can't live without her boyfriend	Li pa ka viv san mennaj li a
She does not want to tell me where	Li pa vle di M ki bò
She doesn't want to leave her kid behind	Li pa vle kite pitit li dèyè
Walk next to me	Mache bò kote M
Who do you think will get there first?	Ki ès ou panse k ap rive an premye?

Extended Adverbs

Fèk translates to "*just*" and is one of those words that has a lot of usage; it behaves the same as its English counterpart in that it precedes the verb.

English	Kreyòl
all	tout *[toot]*
almost	prèske, manke *[mahN-ke]*
already	deja *[dey-zhah]*
always	toujou *[too-zhoo]*
any, nothing	pyès *[pee-es]*
because	paske *[pahs-key]*
being late	an reta *[ahN-rey-tah]*
despite, in spite of	malgre *[mahl-grey]*
not yet	pako, poko *[pah-koh]*
didn't yet	patko, potko *[path-koh]*
early	bonè *[boh-ne]*
especially	espesyalman *[eys-pey-see-ahl-mahN]*
everything	tout bagay *[toot-bah-gah y]*
for	pou *[poo]*
in good health	an sante *[ahN-sahN-tey]*
just	fèk *[fek]*
like, as	tankou *[than-koo]*
mostly	sitou *[see-too]*
never	janm *[jahNm]*
in addition	an plis de *[ahN-plees-dey]*
only	sèlman *[sel-mahN]*
other	lòt *[let]*
prefer, would rather	pito *[pee-toh]*
since	depi *[dey-pee]*
sincerely	sensèman *[sehN-se-mahN]*
so	donk, alò *[ah-lo]*
surely	siman *[see-mahN]*
then	epi *[ey-pee]*
together	ansanm *[ahN-sahNm]*

too much	twòp *[twop]*
too, also	tou *[too]*
very, a lot, many	anpil *[ahN-peel]*

Extended Adjectives

Gran, miyò, cho, vye, fyè, and **chè** are all adjectives that will most likely come up one way or another. Let's take a look at their meanings and also use them in some sentences.

English	Kreyòl
bad	mal *[mahl]*
better	mye, miyò *[mee-yo]*
big	gran *[grahN]*
bitter	amè *[ah-me]*
bright, to light up	klere *[kley-rey]*
clear	klè *[kle]*
cold	fret *[fret]*
empty	vid *[veed]*
expensive	chè *[she]*
full	plen *[plehN]*
hot	cho *[shoh]*
hungry	grangou *[grahN-goo]*
ice cold	glase *[glah-sey]*
old	vye *[vee-ey]*
proud	fyè *[fee-e]*
serious	serye *[sey-ree-ey]*
sick	malad *[mah-lahd]*
strong, smart, loud	fò *[fo]*
sweet	dous, sikre *[doos]*
thirsty	swaf *[swahf]*
tired	fatige *[fah-tee-gey]*
weak	fèb *[feb]*
young	jèn *[zhen]*

These sentences are mostly designed to help those in the medical industry to communicate with their patients. You'll also find some example phrases to help the parents of adoptive children.

English	Kreyòl
I'm not well at all	M pa bon ditou
I don't feel well	M pa santi M byen
We're proud of you	Nou fyè de ou
They aren't so bad	Yo pa twò mal
They aren't in such good health	Yo pa fin twò an sante
It's too expensive	Sa a twò chè
He's sick	Li malad
Are you hot?	Ou cho?
I'm not hot	Mwen pa cho
She's always cold	Li toujou frèt
I'm not hungry	Mwen pa grangou
I'm not thirsty yet	M poko swaf
We're all tired	Nou tout fatige
The Haiti fare is high, especially in the summer	Tikè Ayiti a chè, espesyalman an ete
Make way, let me go	Ranje kò W, ban M pase
She loves all her kids	Li renmen tout pitit li yo
The sun is hot	Solèy la cho
The moon is bright	La lin nan klere
He doesn't want to tell his mom how he feels	Li pa vle di manman L ki jan L santi L
They don't know why she's crying	Yo pa konn pou ki L ap kriye
We know where he is	Nou konn ki kote L ye
His dad won't mind	Papa L pap gen pwoblèm
She doesn't respect anyone	Li pa respekte pyès moun
I can't understand what he says	Mwen pa ka konprann sa L di
She understands everything I say	Li konprann tout sa M di
We just started learning Creole	Nou fèk kòmanse aprann Kreyòl
We've become Creole experts	Nou fin tounen ekspè nan Kreyòl
I don't know how to speak Creole yet	Mwen pako konn pale Kreyòl
We practice Creole every day	Nou pratike Kreyòl chak jou

The kids are at soccer practice	Ti moun yo al nan antrenman foutbòl
The whole family is learning Creole	Tout fanmi an ap aprann Kreyòl
Wait for us at the school	Ret tann nou nan lekòl la
Fhey're playing in the school yard	Y ap jwe nan lakou lekòl la
It's time you teach the kids to drive	Li lè pou W montre ti moun yo kondi
She's never going back to New York	Li pap janm retounen Nou Yòk
The cola is cold	Kola a glase
The beer isn't cold	Byè a pa glase
The beer is colder than the coke	Byè a pi glase pase koka a
The water isn't that cold	Dlo a pa pi glase pase sa
There's nothing left	Pa gen pyès ki rete

The following sentences are great for siblings and adoptive parents to communicate with new members of the family who don't yet speak English. Some adoptive parents choose to learn Creole to communicate with their adoptive kids in their native tongue. They judge that it's important for the kids to continue to use the language, knowing that if they don't use it, they'll eventually forget it. It's a win-win situation where the parents and siblings learn a new language while the adopted children remain connected to their culture.

English	Kreyòl
I'm sleepy	M anvi dòmi
They need some rest	Yo bezwen repo
We go to Haiti every summer	N al Ayiti chak ete
We go to Haiti every July	N antre Ayiti chak mwa Jiyè
He prefers not to eat	Li pito pa manje
They haven't eaten yet	Yo poko manje
They aren't eating yet	Yo poko ap manje
You can take all of it	Ou mèt pran tout
Can we go play?	Ès ke nou mèt al jwe?
You can play with them	Ou mèt jwe avèk yo
She doesn't want to play with me	Li pa vle jwe avè M
She took it without asking	Li pran L san L pa mande
Go take a bath	Al benyen
Go get dressed	Al abiye W
Go brush your teeth	Al bwose dan W
Let me comb your hair	Ban M penyen W
Let him brush your hair	Kite L bwose tèt ou
Kick the ball	Shoute boul la
Kick the ball hard	Shoute boul la fò
Throw it to me	Voye L ban mwen
Can I hold the doll?	M ka kenbe poupe a?
Can I play with the doll?	M ka jwe a poupe a?
I'm combing my doll's hair	M ap penyen tèt poupe M nan
Do you love your doll?	Ou renmen poupe W la?
This is the gift I bought you	Men kado M achte pou ou
Honey, I brought you a gift	Cheri, M achte on kado pou ou
What's your baby's name?	Ki non bebe W la?

Word Search

Search the Kreyòl equivalents in the word search below.

```
K   M   W   E   N   S   Z   B   N   S   E   H   G   M   A
Q   O   G   O   O   Q   M   N   E   W   F   S   A   F   Q
Z   J   N   U   N   E   O   B   N   V   F   C   N   S   C
L   J   N   N   C   T   J   A   U   A   H   L   C   A   O
E   V   I   R   E   D   A   O   O   E   T   P   W   N   P
N   O   S   O   D   N   T   E   T   P   J   I   A   Z   Z
A   P   R   A   N   N   S   Z   E   F   I   N   D   F   U
E   Z   E   H   M   X   A   E   R   E   D   N   A   M   L
R   F   L   H   N   E   N   V   E   B   E   B   L   U   G
P   Q   V   P   T   Y   A   F   I   D   S   Q   F   N   P
A   R   G   P   C   A   N   D   A   V   K   E   C   R   U
Y   S   O   P   K   D   V   G   D   J   K   P   A   G   B
C   D   T   L   T   O   A   A   M   D   I   N   O   E   H
A   N   T   D   Z   B   N   V   J   J   T   Y   E   U   N
N   O   U   M   A   W   T   B   V   X   E   K   Z   Q   D
```

AFTER	ASHAMED	BEFORE
FOR	I	IN
ON	SOUND	TO ADOPT
TO ARRIVE	TO ASK	TO COME BACK
TO KNOW	TO LEARN	TO LEAVE
TO LIVE	TO LOOK	TO TAKE
TO THINK	TO WAIT	TO WALK
TO WANT	WE	WITHOUT

15- US State Abbreviations that are Also Kreyòl Words

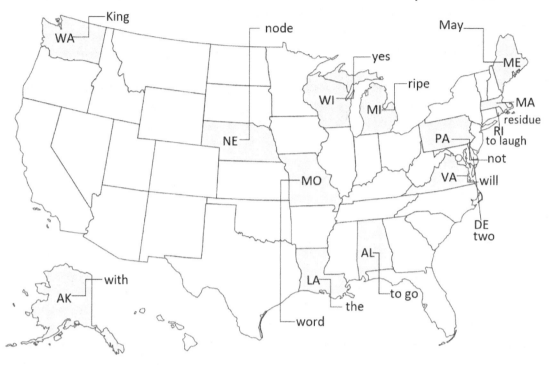

U. S. State Abbreviation/Kreyòl	Translation
AK (Abbreviation for Avèk)	with
AL (Abbreviation for Ale)	to go
DE	two
LA	the
MA	rest, residue, I will
MI	wall, ripe
MO	word
NE	node
PA	not
RI	to laugh
VA	will
WA	King, you
WI	yes

By introducing the "grave" accent, in ME (Main), MO (Missouri), and NE (Nebraska), we end up with three more words:

State Abbreviation/Kreyòl	R2R	Translation
Mè	ME	old lady, sea
Mò	MO	dead person
Nè	NE	nerve

We can even compose some meaningful sentences made up of those two-letter words that are spelled like the two-letter State names.

English	Kreyòl
Don't laugh	Pa ri
You let me know	Wa fè M konnen
The sea is calm	La mè a kalm
Yes, I'll wait for you	Wi, M ap tann ou
Yes, I see what you mean	Wi, Mwen wè sa W vle di
I'll come and get you	Ma vin pran W
I'll come look for them	Ma vin chèche yo
Why don't you take it if you can	Wa vin pran N si W kapab
Go ahead with the kids	Al devan ak ti moun yo
All the mangoes are ripe	Tout mango yo mi
Don't sit on the wall; it's not safe	Pa chita sou mi an; lit pa pridan
I'm only going to say two words	De mo sèlman M ap di
I'll see how you'll defend yourself	Ma va wè kòman W ap defann ou
Please remove the nodes of the sugar cane	Tanpri retire ne kann nan
The old lady is upset that she can't go to see her deceased relative	La mè a gen nè li pa ka al wè mò a
The king said a few words; then he started laughing	Wa a di de mo epi li pete ri
Follow me, and leave the dead to bury their dead	Suiv mwen, e kite mò yo antere mò yo

16-   Similar Sounding Expressions

There are many more words and expressions in Kreyòl that sound English. These can be conveniently separated into two categories: the most important words for your development in the language, and the less fundamental, but still important examples to further enrich your understanding. When you combine the first group with some of the words you are already familiar with, your ability to construct full sentences increases exponentially.

This section provides ample opportunity for you to use R2R as a memorization technique. Be thorough with your associations so that you can maximize retention as you continue to build your vocabulary.

Kreyòl	Sounds Like	Meaning
ba w	bow (down)	give you
bouch	bush	mouth
cho	show	hot
chou	shoe	dear, cabbage
di	D	to tell
Di L	dill	tell him or her
di M	dim	tell me
di N	dean	tell us
dis	diss	ten
fè l	fell	do it
fi	fee	girl
fò l	fall	he must / she must
fri	free	fried
ka w	cow	your case
kat	cat	four
ke	K	that / tail
ki	key	who / what
ki ès?	key S	who is / what is?
konn	con	to know
li	lee	he / she / it
li sa	lisa	read this
li sa	lisa	it's him / her

liv	leave	book
min	mean	mine (excavation)
moun	moon	people
ou	oo	you (singular)
pi	P	more
pi piti	P P T	smaller (est)
pil	peel	pile, battery
piti	P T	small / little
pou l	pool	for him/her
pou li	pulley	for him / her
sa k	sack	what
samdi, sa m di	sam d	saturday, what i say
sa w di	saudi	what you said
sak	sack	sack
sè l	sell	his / her sister
sèl	sell	salt
senk	sync	five
si	see	if / saw / sure
sik	sick	sugar
sis	sis (sister)	six
sou	sue	on / about
ti	T	small / little
ti fi	T fee	little girl
venn	van	vein
vini	vinny	to come
wi	we	yes
yo	yo	they

You can combine the words from the previous table to make up full sentences. Egzanp:

He said yes	Li di wi
He said no	Li di non
He said maybe	Li di petèt
Yes, he told me he's the youngest (or smallest)	Wi, li di M se li ki pi piti
What did you tell the people?	Ki sa W di moun yo?
What did you tell the kids?	Ki sa W di ti moun yo?
You are the one who knows who did it	Se ou ki konn ki ès ki fè te L
The kids came and told me what you said	Se ti moun yo ki vin di M sa W di
Come and tell me what you said about them	Vin di M sa W di sou yo
Have her come with the kids	Fè L vini ak ti moun you
She must tell me who gave it to you	Fò L di M ki moun ki ba W li
Who knows how to do it?	Ki ès ki konn fè L?
He must know who said it	Fò L konn ki ès ki di L
The girls told her to give you the medication	Se ti medam yo ki di pou L ba W medikaman an

WORD SEARCH

More words that are similar – Find the Kreyòl equivalent

D	J	E	M	J	R	W	F	N	L	R	L
A	Q	E	N	E	B	L	I	A	A	N	T
N	N	J	T	A	U	Q	N	M	M	E	I
E	L	I	P	O	L	E	A	O	E	P	E
R	R	T	F	C	L	P	L	W	J	H	V
E	K	E	U	A	M	P	I	G	A	T	E
C	N	I	S	O	A	T	Z	B	L	G	M
H	F	O	T	L	T	N	E	T	A	V	V
B	Z	B	E	E	X	O	W	U	U	Y	F
E	H	C	I	N	Y	W	Q	Y	F	O	S
M	M	W	F	M	Y	G	B	J	K	Z	S
X	K	G	I	A	J	R	R	V	T	E	M

BETWEEN	TO GIVE	TOOTH
TO FINALIZE	BUNCH	ROTTEN
TO LEAVE	ARMY	HAND
TO PUT	TO LICK	AUGUST
TO SPEAK	BREAD	TO STEP ON
TO IMPOUND	TO RETIRE	ALL
ROMAN	ASHAMED	SALTY

17- Kangaroo Words

Some Kreyòl words are made up of the same letters as their English equivalent. However, because Kreyòl words are typically shorter primarily because of the lack of silent letters, the English words tend to have a few more letters and end up carrying their Kreyòl counterparts. We refer to these as kangaroo words. Pa egzanp **Bib** is carried by Bible as being the first 3 letters of Bible. A couple rare exceptions where the Kreyòl word carries the English are the verb *"to detest,"* which means **deteste**, and *"to plan,"* which means **planifye**.

English	Kreyòl
adorable	adorab [*ah-doh-rahb*]
bible	bib [*beeb*]
to detest	deteste [*dey-tey s-tey*]
idea	ide [*ee-dey*]
language	lang [*lahNg*]
letter	lèt [*let*]
notable	notab [*noh-tahb*]
one	on [*ohN*]
plan	planifye [*plah-nee-fee-ey*]
potable	potab [*poh-tahb*]
rare	ra [*rah*]
rest	rès [*res*]
terrible	terib, tèrib [*te-reeb*]
to arrange	ranje* [*rahN-zhey*]
to arrive, to get there	rive [*ree-vey*]
to detest	deteste [*dey-teys-tey*]
to engrave	grave [*grah-vey*]
to plan	planifye [*plah-nee-fee-ey*]

*The soft **g** sound is always represented by the letter **j** and sounds even softer [*zh*]

Sample Sentences

English	Kreyòl
I read my Bible every morning; how about you?	Mwen li bib mwen chak maten, e ou menm?
Who packed the suitcase?	Ki ès ki ranje malèt la?
It was my husband who packed the suitcase for me	Se mari M ki te ranje malèt la pou mwnen
This event will always be engraved in my memory	Evenman sa a ap toujou ret grave nan memwa M
She's going to adopt a child in Haiti	Li pwal adopte on ti moun Ayiti
We are sitting in the first row	Nou chita nan premye ranje a
We were the first to get there	Se nou ki te rive an premye
This is the last time I'm going to let that happen	Se dènye fwa pou M kite sa rive
Are you all almost there?	Ès ke nou prèske rive?
It's very rare that I travel during the month of February	Li ra anpil pou M vwayaje nan mwa Fevriye
They act as if they don't know what they're doing	Yo aji tankou yo pa konn sa Y ap fè
The doctor doesn't know yet when you'll go into labor	Doktè a poko konnen ki lè W ap akouche
Do you know what time it is?	Ès ke W konn ki lè L ye
I don't need to know what you are saying	Mwen pa bezwen konnen sa W ap rankonte a
He fixed everything neatly	Li ranje tout bagay byen pwòp
The baby is adorable	Ti bebe a adorab
He writes his girlfriend a letter every day	Li ekri mennaj li on lèt chak jou
What language are you speaking	Ki lang W ap pale la a?
The cookie cost me a dollar	Bonbon an koute M on dola
Leave the rest for later	Kite rès la pou pi ta
He said a terrible thing about our country	Li di on bagay grav sou peyi nou an
He acts like someone who detests us	Li pale tankou on moun ki deteste nou
I have no idea what he's talking about	M pa gen on ide de sa L ap pale a

Li vini chak samdi

Earlier we saw words like **yè, jodi a, demen, apre demen**; I'm almost certain you'll also have the need to use terms like later, in two days, in a few weeks, in a few years, and others. Don't confuse **lòt** and **lòtre** that appear to follow the same pattern as certain words that are abbreviated such as **vin** and **vini**, which mean *"to come"* and **pot** and **pote**, which mean *"to carry."* **Lòtre** and **lòt** are opposite of each other. **Lòtre jou** means **the other day**, which is in the past, while **lòt semèn** means next week, which is in the future.

There are two different ways of saying next week, month, or year and they are used interchangeably. The first one is **lòt** followed by year, month or week, and the second one is: **k ap vini an**: like in **lòt semèn** or **semèn k ap vini an**.

Yesterday, Tomorrow / Yè, Demen			
Kreyòl	**English**	**Kreyòl**	**English**
jou	day	semèn	week
mwa	month	ane	year
jodi a	today	pi ta	later
demen	tomorrow	apre demen	day after tomorrow
yè	yesterday	avan yè	the other day
lòt semèn	next week	lòtre jou	the other day
semèn k ap vini an	next week	semèn pase	last week
lòt mwa a	next month	mwa pase	last month
kèk jou de sa	a few days ago	nan kèk semèn	in a few weeks
sa gen kèk mwa	it's been a few months	kèk ane de sa	a few years ago
kounyè a	now	pa kounyè a	not now
on sèl fwa	only one time	anpil fwa	often
chak jou	every day	kèk tan	some time, a while

English	Kreyòl
They come to see me every day	Yo vin wè M chak jou
Do you go to school every day?	Ès ke W ale lekòl chak jou?
He's going to the hospital day after tomorrow	Li pwal lopital la aprè demen

They came the other day	Yo te vini lòtre jou
They arrived yesterday	Yo rive yè
They're leaving tomorrow	Y ap pati demen
We're traveling next week	N ap vwayaje lòt semèn
She's giving birth next month	L ap akouche mwa k ap vini a
They go to church every Sunday	Y al legliz chak Dimanch
I'm going to Haiti next month	Mwen pwal Ayiti lòt mwa
I'll be there for a few months	M ap pase kèk mwan
I'm coming back in June	M ap tounen an Jen
It's been a whie since I've been	Mwen gen kèk tan M pa ale

18-   The Numbers

Similar to the vocabulary we've seen so far, there are some words that sound like Creole numbers when they're pronounced in English. They can be easily pronounced using the Kreglish methodology.

Numbers that sound like English

cat	sink	sis	set
4	5	6	7
kat	senk	sis	sèt

dis	dues
10	12
dis	douz

van cat	van sink	van sis	van set
24	25	26	27
venn kat	venn senk	venn sis	venn sèt

Here's a sentence you can also read that makes you sound like a native speaker even if you are a newbie. *Lap Vinny Sam D cat mass*. Notice the similarity with the Kreyòl version: **L ap vini Samdi kat Mas**. You said: She or he's coming Saturday March 4th. I suggest you practice by replacing **kat** with all the other numbers on the chart.

Below is another practical example; by now I am sure you have your favorite verbs and nouns you can combine with these numbers to make up additional sentences.

Lap so T Sam D dues mass
sounds like **L ap soti Samdi douz Mas**
and means **He's going out on Saturday March 12th**

Yo vle adopte sis ti moun	They want to adopt 6 kids
Klas la gen venn sèt elèv	There are 27 students in the classroom
Chak semèn gen sèt jou	There are 7 days in every week
Chak ane gen douz mwa	There are 12 months in every year
Chak ane gen kat sezon	There are 4 seasons in every year
Ti bebe a fèt a dis dwèt li	The baby was born with all 10 fingers

Zewo (0) is a cognate where **r** is replaced with **w**. Below are the numbers 1 through 10 that are a little bit harder to pronounce. However, I'm confident that you've come a long way and can now pronounce them. If not, I'll continue to guide you along with plenty of opportunities to practice. I know you aren't far off and will reach your goal in no time.

1 through 10

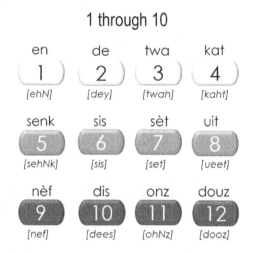

en	de	twa	kat
1	2	3	4
[ehN]	[dey]	[twah]	[kaht]

senk	sis	sèt	uit
5	6	7	8
[sehNk]	[sis]	[set]	[ueet]

nèf	dis	onz	douz
9	10	11	12
[nef]	[dees]	[ohNz]	[dooz]

Li manje de nan pen yo	She ate 2 pieces of bread
Li gen twa jou li pa manje	She hasn't eaten in 3 days
N ap vwayaje nan kat jou	We're traveling in 4 days
Ane a ap fini nan senk semèn	The year will be over in 5 weeks

Below are a few differences between Kreyòl and English numbers.

- In the numeral and decimal forms, the commas and periods are reversed.
  - In English this is: 1,250.90
  - In Kreyòl that would be: 1.250,90

- In Kreyòl, one is omitted before hundred or thousand, but not before million. Those numbers are simply known as:
  - san, which means 100
  - mil, which means 1,000
  - on milyon, which means 1,000,000

- The direct translation for 1 is **en**; however **on, yon** or **youn** is used in a sentence. Pa egzanp:
  - **Li prete M on dola**   She loaned me one dollar

122

- o **Di on priyè pou mwen**   Say a prayer for me
- o **Ba L youn**   Give her one
- The adjectives or nouns following the numbers whether it's one or many don't have the plural mark; they remain in the singular form.
  - o **On dola**   One dollar
  - o **De prezidan**   Two presidents
  - o **Dis bato**   Ten boats
  - o **Onz million moun**   Eleven million people

Ordinal numbers are formed by adding the suffix **-yèm** to the cardinal number, except in the case of *first* (**premye**). On the other end of the spectrum, *last* is **dènye**. Prior to adding the suffix to:

- **de** and **twa**, **z** is introduced: **dezyèm, twazyèm**
- **kat**, **r** is introduced: **katryèm**
- **sis** and **dis**, the ending **s** changes to **z**: **sizyèm, dizyèm**
- **sèt**, the accented **è** changes to the regular **e** without the accent: **setyèm**
- **nèf,** the accented **è** changes to the regular **e** and **f** becomes **v**: **nevyèm**

Numbers				
	Cardinal		Ordinal	
Number	Kreyòl	English	Kreyòl	English
1	en	one	premye	first
2	de	two	dezyèm	second
3	twa	three	twazyèm	third
4	kat	four	katryèm	fourth
5	senk	five	senkyèm	fifth
6	sis	six	sizyèm	sixth
7	sèt	seven	setyèm	seventh
8	uit	eight	uityèm	eighth
9	nèf	nine	nevyèm	ninth
10	dis	ten	dizyèm	tenth

Sa fè dezyèm ti moun yo adopte   This is the second child they've adopted

Senatè a sou katriyèm tèm ni	The senator is in her fourth term
Se pa premye fwa M vin isi a	This isn't the first time I come here
M pwal nan kenzyèm etaj	I'm going to the fifteenth floor
Prezidan an ap pran on dènye kesyon	The president will take one last question
Dènye fwa a se pa t sa L te di	That's not what he said the last time
Premye Janvye se Dat Endepandans	January first is Independence Day
Premye Janvye se on dat enpòtan	January first is an important date
nan istwa peyi Ayiti	in Haitian history

Part III

The Alphabet / Alfabè

In the next few pages, I will introduce words that begin or end with each letter of the Kreyòl alphabet and are spelled exactly the same or very similarly in both languages. This resource isn't meant to be a dictionary because our primary focus is on words that are similar, therefore easier to memorize. Amongst those you are sure to encounter common words that help bring you closer to the quantity required for basic and even advanced konvèsasyon. In addition, you will also learn short two-letter words that consist of a vowel and a consonant (pa egzanp, the **ap** and **pa** that you saw earlier). There are over a dozen of those two-letter words with each vowel except the letter **ò** where there's fewer. Some of those words play an important role in the language and are relatively easy to remember. If you use R2R and relate them to acronyms that you're already familiar with, then you're sure to retain them for good.

KREYÒL ALPHABET
Know the sounds of the letters and blends
Especially the vowels

(A) (B) (C) (D)   two vowels never follow each other except: ou & ui. In any other case, they're separated by y. Example: Kreyòl, peyi

y + vowel replaces i + vowel

(E) (È) (F) (G)

(A) There's little difference in the consonant sounds. Beginners should focus on the vowel sounds that are key to pronunciation.

(CH) (Y+v) (AN)

(H) (I) (J) (K)   (x) x & q don't exist

(L) (M) (N) (O)   There's a 1 to 1 relationship between each sound and each letter or blend. The sound K is represented by letter K only and never by the numerous letters or combos that English uses, such as hard c, ch, q, qu.

(OU) (KS) (EN)   Nasals n is silent

(Ò) (P) (Q) (R)

(UI) (GZ) (ON)

(S) (T) (U) (V)   If you can read or write in any Latin based language, all you need to read and write Kreyòl is packed in this single slide

(IN)   Same Sound as English

(W) (X) (Y) (Z)   c & h are always together   (c)   u is always paired with either o or i

Due to the phonetic characteristic of Kreyòl, there are some differences in the Kreyòl alphabet worth mentioning. There are two letters of the English alphabet that don't exist in Kreyòl and they are **Q** and **X**. **C** and **H** are never seen apart from each other **because H** always follows **C**

126

like with **match**, which is also Kreyòl. **U** is not a vowel as you know it since it's never seen alone. It's always either followed by **I** or it follows **O** like **nuit** meaning "night" and **tout** meaning "all."

G always has the hard sound similar to English while **J** makes an even softer sound than the one as pronounced in the name "Jane." It sounds more like **ZH**. Pa egzanp, in **garaj** which is the equivalent of "garage," the **J** sounds more like garazh. Other than those exceptions listed above, all the other consonants are pronounced the same within a word. The main difference in terms of pronunciation as mentioned very early on is the pronunciation of the vowels.

The nasals which we'll see at the end of this section, are arguably the most difficult to sound out in Kreyòl. You had an opportunity to practice pronouncing them earlier and there'll be more opportunities moving forward as I introduce you to more words that are spelled identically to some English words that you know.

19-   THE LETTER A (LÈT A)

A [*ah*] shorten the sound; do not pronounce the **h**

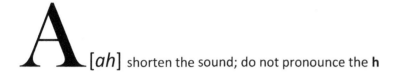

A	means	The
Mango a [*mahN-goh*]	means	The mango

The letter **a** in Kreyòl is always pronounced as the **a** in the word "*water*," except when it is followed by **n,** it becomes a nasal sound.

For almost every letter (**lèt**), there is a group (**gwoup**) of words with identical (**idantik**) spellings and meanings, but different (**diferan**) pronunciations (**pwononsyasyon**). These words may also represent (**reprezante**) any part (**pati**) of speech. Since they are so varied (**varye**), you can immediately (**imedyatman**) start combining (**konbine**) them to create (**kreye**) sentences, which we will do after the **chak** section (**seksyon**).

Since you've mastered pronunciation by now, the goal now is to extend your vocabulary by taking advantage (**avantaj**) of the great number words that are spelled exactly (**egzakteman**) or pretty close to some words in English. The words that aren't cognates have different meanings despite the similarity in spelling. It helps to continue to use R2R to improve memorization. If you require more help with pronunciation, you can watch the videos on my blog at haiti2030.org or on my YouTube channel.

"A" Words with Identical Spelling and Meaning

Kreyòl	English
admire [ahd-mee-rey]	to admire
adore [ah-doh-rey]	to adore
agonize [ah-goh-nee-zey]	to agonize
arab [ah-rahb]	arab
aspirin [ahs-pee-reen]	aspirin

Sample Sentences – A

Kreyòl	English
Tout moun admire madanm sa a pou travay li fè	Everyone admires this lady for the work she does
Mwen adore bon Dye ki se sèl sovè M	I adore God who is my only savior
Yo pa ka gade ti pitit la k ap agonize nan eta sa a	They cannot bear to watch the little kid agonizing in this manner
Li pran aspirin nan deja	She already took the aspirin
Li bon pou ou pran on grenn aspirin chak jou	It's good to take one aspirin per day

"A" Words with Same Spelling but Different Meaning

Kreyòl	English
a [ah]	the, with, at, on (a lè)
al (short for ale) [ahl]	to go
ale [ah-ley]	to go
aspire [ahs-pee-rey]	to inhale

Similar to English, two of the shortest words in Kreyòl are *a* and *an*. Interestingly enough, they play an almost identical (**idantik**) role (**wòl**) in these two languages. In English, they are indefinite articles and precede the noun while in Kreyòl, they are two of six singular definite articles, but they succeed the noun. They are also sometimes paired with a second definite article. For example, *le* or *la* like in **le pè a** and **la mè an**, meaning *"the old man"* and *"the old lady"* respectively. There are certain cases where a follows *la*, to indicate (**endike**) or point at something or someone. Pa egzanp, in **mwen pwale la a** means *"I'm going there."* When the letter **a** follows *sa,* it's the equivalent of the demonstrative article (**atik**) *this* or *that*. When referring to multiple items, **a** is replaced by **yo** like in **sa yo** which means *"these or those."* This is a very common structure that takes some getting used to. **A** also means *"at"* when telling time or *"on"* in expressions like "on time," which means **a lè**.

Egzanp

Kreyòl	English
bale a	the broom
doktè a	the doctor
elèv sa yo	these students
gran nèg sa yo	those rich people
madanm sa a	this lady
mesye sa a	that man
nèg sa a	this man
pate a	the patty
peyi sa a	that country
ti fi sa a	this little girl
ti gason sa a	that little boy
ti moun sa yo	these kids
tout tan sa a	all that time
yo toujou a lè	they're always on time

Let's use the word "a" in some sentences

Kreyòl	English
L ale la a	He went there
Do a fè M mal	My back hurts
Li manje tout pate a	He ate the whole patty
Lonje bale a pou mwen	Hand me the broom
Li te kanpe nan la ri a	She stood on the street
Li te chita sou galri a	He sat on the front porch
Plen pye bwa nan lakou a	There are lots of trees in the backyard
Ouvri baryè a	Open the gate

Manje a gen bon gou	The food tastes good
Manje sa a on ti jan pike	This food is a little spicy
Direktè a poko rive	The director has not arrived yet
Biwo a fèmen a twa zè	The office closes at three
Fò W rive a lè	You must arrive on time
Lè a fin rive sou nou	The time is upon us
Liv Kreyòl sa a an fòm	This Creole book is excellent
M ap rekòmande W liv Kreyòl sa a	I'll recommend this Creole book
Doktè a pran swen malad la	The doctor takes care of the patient

One and Two-Letter Words – **A**

Kreyòl contains a large number of short words that are relatively easy to remember. I suggest you use the R2R technique to link them to acronyms you're familiar with or two-letter State names we saw earlier. In the case of the letter **A**, there are 19 two-letter words, 5 of which begins with **A**, while the remaining 14 end with a. Due to the phonetic characteristic of Kreyòl where every sound is written only one way, there are many homonyms in the language. As a result some of the words in the one and two-letter charts may have various meanings; however only one translation is displayed on the charts themselves while the others are added to the accompanying tables.   Within the two-letter word charts, the most common words are in the black shapes while the least common are in the grey shapes. Midway through the sentences that follow, you'll see one ending with **anpil anpil**; that's not a typo. It's a common construct in Kreyòl where a word is repeated to stress its importance. It's like *very* followed by an adjective.

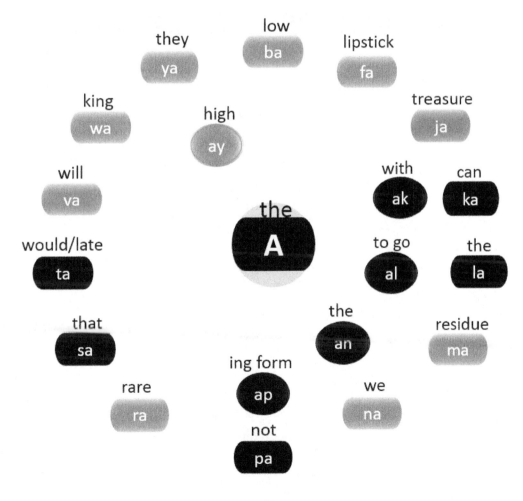

Kreyòl	English
Yo pa ka al pi ta pase wa a	They can't go later than the king
Ki sa L ap fè ak sa?	What's he doing with that?
Li ra pou L rive ta konsa	It's rare for her to arrive so late
Ou jwenn malèt la?	Did you find the suitcase?
Ti pitit la renmen mete fa	The little girl likes to wear lipstick
Yo te jwenn on pakèt ja Ayiti	Lots of treasures were found in Haiti
Li ak papa L sanble anpil anpil	She and her dad look so much alike
Ba L on chans	Give him a chance
M ap rankontre W nan ba a	I'll meet you at the bar
Ou pa wè ba W la chire	Don't you see that your stocking is torn
Sa a pi ba pase lòt la	This one is lower than the other

Two-letter words that either start or end with *a*

Kreyòl	English
ak	with
al (abbreviation for ale)	to go
an	the
ap	ing form
ay	high
ba	bar, low, to give, stocking
fa	lipstick
ja	treasure
ka	can, case
la	the, there
ma	residue, I will
na	we
pa	not, step
ra	rare
sa	that
ta	would, late
va	to go, will
wa	king
ya	they

Konvèsasyon

Mom is waking her son up to get ready for school. But he's tired and asks Mom permission to stay in bed for a few more minutes. Both of them are very polite and affectionate with each other. Which words and expressions will you use in a similar konvèsasyon in the future?

Come on baby it's time to wake up	Cheri li lè pou ou leve
Today is the first day of school	Jodi a se premye jou lekòl
Are you excited to go to school?	Ou kontan ou pwal lekòl?
Yes mom, I am	Wi manman M kontan
Are you happy to wear your new clothes?	Ou kontan W ap mete rad nèf ou yo?
Yes I love them	Wi M renmen yo
Get up, go take a bath	Leve pou W al benyen
I am tired	M fatige
If you don't wake up now, you will be late	Si W pa leve kounyè a, W ap an reta
Can I sleep for a few more minutes?	M ka fè on ti dòmi ankò?
OK, you have five more minutes	OK, ou gen senk minit ankò
What do you want for breakfast?	Kisa W vle manje pou dejene?
I want cereal Mom	M vle sereyal manmi
I have a headache	Tèt mwen ap fè M mal
Take this aspirin, and you'll feel better	Pran aspirin sa a, epi W ap santi W miyò
Thank you Mom	Mèsi manmi
I adore you my darling	Mwen adore W cheri
Me too Mom I love you too	Mwen tou manmi mwen renmen W tou

20-   THE LETTER B (LÈT B)

B [*bey*] shorten the sound and do not pronounce the **y**.

Consonants (**konsòn yo**) sound virtually the same in both languages (**lang**). But another characteristic (**karakteristik**) of Kreyòl is that many words that end with a silent vowel in French or English end with a consonant, leaving out the silent letters. This is evidence (**evidans**) of how much simpler (**pi senp**) Kreyòl spelling is, compared (**konpare**) to those other languages. As a native English speaker, you may not perceive the ending **le** of the words below as complex. However, for someone being introduced to the language for the first time, it can definitely (**definitivman**) represent (**reprezante**) a challenge. The absence of **le** in those words, makes them simpler to read and pronounce.

Kreyòl	English
bib *[beeb]*	bible
kab *[kahb]*	cable
kapab *[kah-pahb]*	capable
doub *[doob]*	double
enkwayab *[ehN-kwah-yahb]*	incredible
enposib *[ehN-poh-seeb]*	impossible
envensib *[ehN-vehN-seeb]*	invincible
envizib *[ehN-vee-zeeb]*	invisible
nòb *[nob]*	noble
posib *[poh-seeb]*	possible
responsab *[rey-spohN-sahb]*	responsible

rezonab *[rey-zoh-nahb]*	reasonable
tab *[tahb]*	table
twoub *[twoob]*	trouble
vizib [vee-*zeeb*]	visible

"B" Words with Identical Spellings and Meanings

Kreyòl	English
bank *[bahNk]*	bank
baton *[bah-tohN]*	baton
bravo *[brah-voh]*	bravo

Sample Sentences – B

Kreyòl	English
Ès ke nou pwal la bank la demen?	Are you all going to the bank tomorrow?
Polisye a bat volè a avèk on baton	The policeman beat the thief with a baton
Li pa ka manche san banton ankò	He can no longer walk without a cane
Se pa tout moun ki bat bravo pou senatè a	It's not everyone who claps for the senator

"B" Words with Same Spelling but Different Meaning

Kreyòl	English
bag *[bahg]*	ring
bale *[bah-ley]*	broom, to sweep
ban *[bahN]*	bench, let, to give
bay *[by]*	to give, goodbye
bare *[bah-rey]*	to block, to catch, to corner
bat *[baht]*	to beat
bit *[beet]*	pile
bite *[bee-tey]*	to stumble
blaze *[blah-zey]*	faded
bone *[boh-ney]*	bonnet, beanie hat
bout *[boot]*	piece
bra *[brah]*	arm

Sample Sentences – B

Kreyòl	English
Li achte on bag an dyaman pou mennaj li a	He brought a diamond ring for his girlfriend
Tanpri pran bale a pou mwen	Please take the broom for me
Ou ka lonje bale a pou mwen?	Can you hand me the broom?
Ou bale kay la pi byen pase M	You sweep the house better than I
Li pa ban M pwoblèm	I am not troubled by it (literally: It does not give me any problems)
Men L chita sou ban an	Here she is, sitting on the bench
Nenpòt ki jan mwen pap bay le gen	No matter what I am not giving up
Men W bare L; li pa ka wè anyen	Your hand is in her way; she can't see anything
Bit tè a monte pi wo pase kay la	The pile of dirt is higher than the house
Nou bite men N pa tonbe	We stumble but we do not fall
Ti rad la blaze men li fè ti madanm nan byen	The little dress is faded but it looks good on the little girl
Ti bebe Ayisyen toujou met bone, paske manman yo pè pou yo pa pran refwadisman	Haitian babies always wear a beanie hat, because their mother fears without it, they would catch a cold
M grangou tanpri ban M on bout pen	I am hungry, please give me a piece of bread
Lage bra M	Let go of my arm
Doktè a ba L on piki nan bra	The doctor gave him a shot in his arm

Another interesting similarity between the two languages is the number of words that are not only perfect anagrams for each other, but also translate each other. This is yet another great example of the greater relative closeness of Kreyòl to English than French. Because of the complexity present in French writing, the equivalent word for **boat** is "*bâteau*," which doesn't have much in common with the English equivalent and the word **law** in French which is "*loi*." Although the French and Kreyòl words sound the same, their spelling is quite different.

Kreyòl	English
bato *[bah-toh]*	boat
lwa *[lwah]*	law

Sample Sentences – B

Kreyòl	English
Malere yo pran bato pou Y al lòt bò	The poor soul got on makeshift boats to try and make it abroad
Mwen pa renmen monte bato paske M pa konn naje	I don't like getting on boats because I don't know how to swim
M achte on jwèt bato pou li pou fèt li	I bought a toy boat for him for his birthday
Motè bato a sispann mache	The motor of the boat stopped running

"B" Words with Slightly Different Spellings

The words in the table below are spelled slightly differently between the two languages. "Be" in the middle column has nothing to do with the Kreyòl word **bè** in terms of meaning. My suggestion is to use it as a memory aid. Pa egzanp, **butter** may be thought of as *"be"* with an added grave accent.

In the first row below, you can see the similarity between *ba L* and ***ball*** in *Ba L which means "**Give him**"* You simply need to think of *the ball as the object being given as the reminder.*

Kreyòl	Similar Spelling	Meaning
ba l	ball	give him
bandi	bandit	bandit
bè	be	butter
blese	bless	to bleed
bonè or bone	bone	beanie hat
bòl	bowl	bowl
bòykote	boycott	to boycott
bway (borrowed from english)	boy	boy

While the preceding words are similar in spelling, the ones that follow sound similar.

Kreyòl	Similar Sound	Meaning
bèl	belle	beautiful
bèt	bet	animal, beast
bòs	boss	boss
bòt	but	boots
bòykòt	boycott	boycott
bòy	boy	flour dough

Konvèsasyon

The folks below are introducing themselves to each other and talking about their profession as well as the importance of holding a job.

Bonjou kòman ou ye?	Good morning how are you?
Mwen an fòm	I am well
E ou menm?	How about you?
Mwen pa pi mal	I am not bad
Kòman ou rele?	What's your name?
Mwen rele Sebhastien	My name is Sebhastien
E ou menm, ki non W?	How about you, what's your name?
M rele Lynda	My name is Lynda
M kontan fè konesans ou	I am pleased to meet you
Pale M de ou	Tell me about you
Kisa W fè kòm travay	What do you do?
Mwen se pwofesè e ou menm?	I'm a teacher and you?
Mwen se chofè	I'm a driver
Ou renmen djòb ou a?	Do you like your job?
Men wi mwen renmen N	Yes I like it
Se avè L M peye lekòl ti moun yo	It helps me pay the kids' tuition
Mwen di Bon Dye mèsi li ban M travay sa a	I thank God I have a job
Gen moun ki pa genyen ditou	There are some who don't have a job
Mwen menm tou M konsidere ke M gen chans M ap travay	I also consider myself fortunate to have a job

21- THE LETTER C (LÈT C)

C [*sey*] shorten the sound. Do not pronounce the **y**.

C is one of 3 special letters (*c, h, and u*) that only exists in paired form in Kreyòl. The letter *c* is always fllowed by **h**. In English, there is the soft **c** sound like in *cent, scene, city* or *cigar*, and the hard **k** sound as seen in *car, couple or cut*. We find both the soft and hard sound in *circle*. As mentioned earlier, there can only be a one to one relationship between a letter or blend and a sound. As a result, *c* isn't used for any of the aforementioned sounds, *s* is a more natural fit for the soft sound while *k* is a better fit for the hard sound. As a result, there're no **c** words without an **h**.

Another prevalent sound is produced when *c* is paired with *h* to make a relatively "hard" sound like in *reach* or *child*. In Kreyòl, the *ch* sound is of the softer variety like in *ship* and *shoe*. The harder sound that matches the English is made only when *ch* is preceded by **t**.

"Ch" Words with Same Spelling and Meaning

Kreyòl	English
match	match

Sample sentences – CH

Kreyòl	English
Match la rèd	The game is tight
Ès ke ou pwal nan match la?	Are you going to the game?

Nou rive nan fen match la	We are at the end of the game
Nou ka pèdi match la men nou pap pèdi chanpyona a	We may lose the game but we won't lose the championship

"C" Words with Same Spellings but Different Meanings

Kreyòl	**English**
chase *[shah-sey]*	to hunt, to kick out

"C" Words with Slightly Different Spelling

Kreyòl	English
echalòt *[ey-shah-lot]*	shallot
chas *[shahs]*	to go hunting
Chasè *[shah-se]*	Hunter

Sample sentences – C

Kreyòl	English
Li pa renmen chase	He doesn't like to hunt
Medikaman an chase maladi a	The medication chased the disease away
Te a chase mal tèt la	The tea chased the headache away
Manzè sa a se on bon chasè	This lady is a good hunter
L al la chas chak wikenn	She goes hunting every weekend
La chas se on pasyon pou li	Hunting is a passion of hers

Konvèsasyon

A mother and her son are having a konvèsasyon where Mom asks about Dad's whereabouts and whether the kid knows when Dad will come home.

Kote papa W?	Where's your dad?
L al la chas	He went hunting
Papa W pat di M li t ap soti non	Your dad didn't tell me he was going out
M pa konnen	I don't know
Depi ki lè L soti?	When did he go out?
Menm kote W soti a maten an	As soon as you left this morning
Li pat di W ki lè L ap vini?	Did he tell you when he'll be back?
Non li pa t di M	No he didn't tell me
Kisa L al chase a menm?	What's he hunting?
A, mwen pa fouti di W	Ah, I couldn't tell you
Gen lè se zwazo	He may be hunting birds
Papa W fin tounen chasè pwofesyonèl	Your dad has become a professional hunter
Sanble sa	It seems like it
M ap vini, M pwal nan mache	I'll be back, I'm going to the market place
Sa W ap achte pou mwen manmi?	What will you buy me Mom?
Sa W vle cheri?	What do you want honey?
Fè M sipriz	Surprise me
OK, M konn ki sa M ap achte pou ou	OK, I know what I'm going to buy you
M pa ka tann pou M wè sa W ap pote pou mwen	I can't wait to see what you'll bring me
Bay manmi	Bye Mom

22- THE LETTER D (LÈT D)

D [*dey*] shorten the sound. Do not pronounce the y.

As we saw in the beginning, **d** sounds like the Kreyòl word **di** when pronounced in English. Similar to most other consonants, there's no difference between the two languages when **d** is pronounced within a word. When followed by **i**, you need to make one adjustment in terms of pronunciation. Instead of positioning your tongue against the roof of your mouth, you need to place it at the edge of your teeth as you do when you pronounce **c**.

"D" Words with Same Spelling and Meaning

Kreyòl	English
demand *[dey-mahNd]*	demand, request
demon *[dey-mohN]*	demon, devil
divan *[dee-vahN]*	divan, couch
double *[doo-bley]*	to double, to pass

The following examples are Kangaroo words where the English word carries its Kreyòl counterpart.

Kreyòl	English
demoli *[dey-moh-lee]*	to demolish
doub *[doob]*	double (noun)

Sample Sentences - D

Kreyòl	English
Mwen gen on sèl demand	I only have one request
Li mande respè	He asks respect
Dòmi pran L sou divan an	He fell asleep on the divan
Tout machin ki sou wout la double nou	All the cars that are on the road overtook us
Yo ta sipoze demoli kay sa a	They should demolish this house
M ap vin demen bonè bonè	I am coming very early tomorrow
Mwen wè doub (or twoub) dòk	I see double, doc (blurry vision)
Mande L ki sa L santi	Ask him what he feels
Mande L ki jan L santi L	Ask her how she feels

The last two sentences are commonly used by medical professionals to ask atheir patients what they feel via an interpreter. You can begin experimenting by bypassing your interpreter and asking your patient directly:

What do you feel?	**Kisa W santi?**
How do you feel?	**Kòman ou santi W?**

"D" Words with Same Spelling but Different Meaning

Kreyòl	English
dan *[dahN]*	tooth
dig *[deeg]*	pile of mud (farming)
dine *[dee-ney]*	lunch
dire *[dee-rey]*	to last
do *[doh]*	back
don *[dohN]*	gift, aid
doze *[doh-zey]*	to master
drive *[dree-vey]*	to wear good clothes casually

Sample sentences – D

Kreyòl	English
Ou gen on apsè nan dan an	You have an abscess in the tooth
Dan an gate nèt	This tooth is completely rotten
N ap oblije rache dan an	We will have to extract the tooth
Li pap dire tout tan sa a	It won't last that long
Do L frèt	His back feels cold
Li santi on fredi nan do L	His back feels cold
Do M ap fè M mal	My back is hurting
Li fè on don paske li kwè nan kòz la	She made a donation because she believes in the cause
Li doze balon an sou tèt li	She balanced the ball on her head
Li pa drive bèl ti rad li a, li mete L pou okazyon espesyal sèlman	She doesn't wear her beautiful little dress, if it isn't a special occasion
Papa, M renmen lè W pote M sou do	Dad, I like when you give me piggy back rides
Kouche a tè a epi M ap monte sou do W	Lie down on the floor and I'll stand on your back
Ou vle monte sou do M cheri?	Do you want to play horsey, honey?

"D" Words with slightly different spelling

Kreyòl	R2R	Meaning
dat	date	date
dèt	debt	debt
di M	dim	tell me
di L	dill	tell him/her
di N	dean	tell us
dantis	dentist	dentist
danti	denture	denture
dakò	accord	to agree

Konvèsasyon

There's no doubt that people will be curious and question whether or not you speak Kreyòl. We want to make sure you can tell them that you do and provide some additional detail pertaining to how you learned it and how much you know.

Ou pale Kreyòl?	Do you speak Creole?
Mwen ka degaje m wi	I can get by
Ki bò ou aprann ni?	Where did you learn?
M gen lontan m ap vwayaje Ayiti.	I have been traveling to Haiti for a long time
Chak fwa M ale, M aprann on bagay an plis	Every time I go, I learn a little bit more
Ki moun ki aprann ou Kreyòl?	Who taught you Creole?
Zanmi mwen, M gen on pakèt zanmi nan peyi a	My friends, I have lots of friends in the country
Depi konbyen tan W ap antre soti nan peyi a?	How long have you been traveling to Haiti?
Sa fè plis ke di zan.	It's been more than ten years
Kisa W al fè lòt bò a?	What do you do while in Haiti
M fè anpil kalite bagay	I do a lot of different things
Ki kalite bagay konsa?	What kinds of things?
M pa ka di W; si M di W, M ap blije touye W, LOL	I can't tell you; if I do, I'll have to kill you, LOL
Se pa vre mon chè, se blag M ap bay	Not true my friend; I'm only kidding
Ou wè M sanble moun ki konn touye moun?	Do I look like a killer to you?
M pa konnen, si W di M, mwen fèt pou M kwè W	I don't know, if you say it, I have no choice but to believe you

Lèt E

23-   THE LETTER E (LÈT E)

E *[ey]* shorten the sound. Do not pronounce the **y**.

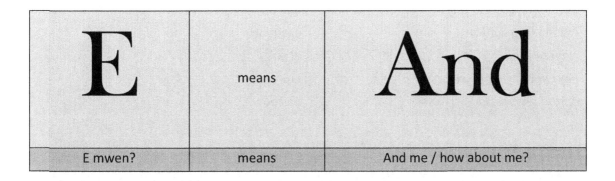

E	means	And
E mwen?	means	And me / how about me?

E is a single letter word with several meanings: "and," "with," "plus," or "how about." It sounds like a long **a** in English.

Those versed in French are prone to write the sound *[ey]* with an accent **é**, which is highly prevalent in French. In Kreyòl, **e** only takes the grave accent when appropriate, but never the sharp accent or accent "aigu." Pa egzanp, the following are all written without the sharp accent:

> **kafe** *[kah-fey]*: coffee.
> **gate** *[gah-tey]*: spoil or rotten.
> **pale** *[pah-ley]*: to speak.
> **pete** *[pey-tey]*: to fart.

"E" Words with Same Spelling and Meaning

elan *[ey-lahN]*   elan, run-up, gather speed

Sample sentence – E

Kreyòl	English
Atlèt la pran elan anvan L kòmanse kouri	The athlete gathers speed before she begins running

"E" Words with Slightly Different Spelling

Kreyòl	English
efò *[ey-fo]*	effort
egal *[ey-gahl]*	equal
egalite *[ey-gah-lee-tey]*	equality
egzanp *[eyg-zahNp]*	example
eko *[ey-koh]*	echo
emosyon *[ey-moh-see-ohN]*	emotion
epizòd *[ey-pee-zod]*	episode

Sample Sentences – E

Kreyòl	English
Ban M on egzanp	Give me an example
Ou tande eko a?	Do you hear the echo?
Li gen anpil emosyon	She is full of emotion

One and Two-Letter Words – E

Besides **E** that's a single letter word, there are 14 two-letter words with **E** out of which **ke, se, te**, and the number **de** are perhaps the most common.

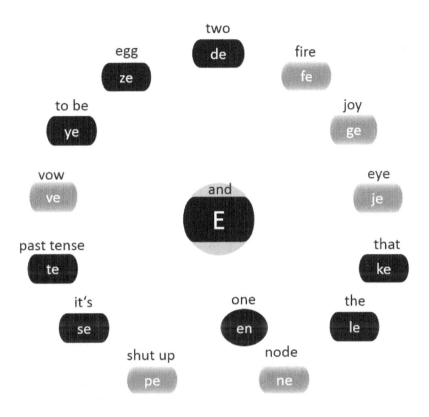

E polisye yo?	How about the policemen?
Se li k pote L	He's the one who brought it
Nou te vle manje ze	We wanted to eat some eggs
Ki jan ou ye?	How are you?
Ki moun ou ye?	Who are you?
Sa yo ye?	What are they?
Sa fè de fwa M di N pou N pe	This is the second time I asked you to be quiet
M pa wè nan je a	I don't see in the eye
A la nou ge jodi a	You guys are so joyful today
Se moun ki toujou ge	That's someone who's always happy
Yo gen tan etèn di fe a	They already put out the fire
Se ve ke L te fè jou maryaj li	That's the vow she made on her wedding day

Kreyòl	English
de	two
fe (di fe)	fire
ge	joy, merriment
je	eye, play
ke	that
le	the
ne	node
pe	to be quiet
se	it's
te	past tense mark, tea
ve	vow
ye	to be
ze	egg

Konvèsasyon

Mom asks her oldest son about his brother and sisters. He takes the opportunity to remind her that his younger brother doesn't listen to him.

Kreyòl	English
Kote medam yo?	Where are the girls?
Mwen pa konnnen	I don't know?
E ti frè W, kote li?	How about your little brother where is he?
M pa wè L depi manten	I haven't seen him since this morning
Li te di W L ap soti?	Did he tell you he was going out?
Non, mwen menm!	Me, no!
Se ou k pi gran	You're the oldest
Ou responsab lè M pa la	You're in charge when I'm not home
Misye pa tande M non, manman	Mom, this guy doesn't listen to me
Lè misye vini Wa fè L sonje sa	When he comes home you can remind him of that
M pap manke	I'll make sure of that
Se si L t ap koute W	If only he would listen
Li bliye fasil	He forgets so easily
Ou vle di li pran pòz bliye L	You mean he pretends to forget
Se egzakteman sa M te vle di	It's exactly what I mean
L ap oblije tande M fwa sa a	He's going to have to listen this time
M espere sa	I hope so

153

24-   THE LETTER È (LÈT È)

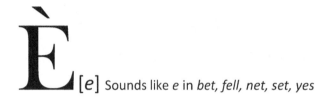

È [e] Sounds like *e* in *bet, fell, net, set, yes*

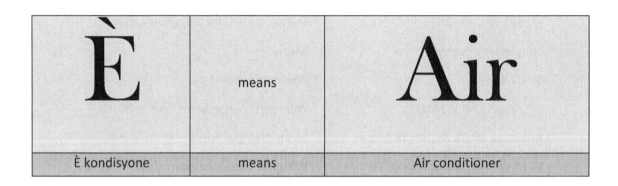

È	means	Air
È kondisyone	means	Air conditioner

È is pronounced exactly like the short *e* in English. You'll see many words with the same spelling and same pronunciation in both languages listed below. The only difference in those cases is the grave accent in the *e* in Kreyòl. Pa egzanp, ***bèt, lèt, nèt, sèt,*** and ***vèt.***

Onè is one with an accent and is part of a traditional Haitian greeting that is one of the most telling examples of the inviting nature of Haitians. Unfortunately, the greeting is not used that much anymore. I would like to encourage everyone to not only start using it again but also to start teaching the world the polite ways of Haitians.

Back in the day, when you visited people's homes you greeted them by yelling ***onè***, which means "honor," as in it's an honor for me to come to your home or I'm honored to be in your presence. The host would reply ***respè***, which means "respect," indicating they respectfully welcomed the visitor. What a wonderful sign of respect from both the guest and the host. It gives me goose bumps just writing it down.

"È" Words with Similar Spelling but Different Meaning

The table below contains a combination of cognates and other words whose spelling is very close to some English words. In most cases, the difference is the accented vowel **è** in Kreyòl. Remember the middle column doesn't always have something to do with the meaning of the word, and sometimes, it's just a suggested memory aid.

Kreyòl	R2R	Meaning
aktè	actor	actor
alfabè	alphabet	alphabet
amè	amen	bitter
amèn	amen	amen
frèt	fret	cold
lèt	let	letter, milk
nèt	net	entire
onè	one	honor
parès	pare	laziness
parèt	pare	to appear
parèy	pare	same
parye	pare	to bet
pyès	piece	none, piece, room
rès	rest	rest
respè	respect	respect
sèt	set	seven
vèt	vet	green
wè	we	to see
wès	west	west

Sample sentences – È

Kreyòl	English
Mwen frèt	I am cold
Li fè frèt Jodi a	It's cold today
È se on lèt enpòtan an Kreyòl	È is an important letter in Creole
Sa a se on lèt damou	This is a love letter
Nenpòt kote ou ye sou planèt la, on semèn toujou genyen sèt jou	Anywhere you are on the planet, there are always seven days in a week
Ou mèt lave tout nèt	You can wash them all
Pou fèt Sen Patrik, fò W met on chemiz vèt	For Saint Patrick's day, you must wear a green shirt
Met tout rès la nan plat mwen an	Put the rest in my plate
Yo pa gen respè pou pyès moun	They don't respect anyone
Ranplase pyès machin sa a	Replace this car part

One and Two-Letter Words – È

Besides **È**, which by itself is a single letter word that means "*air*" and is used to tell time, there are 20 two-letter words with è. The ones in the black shapes like **èd, ès, fè, lè, wè,** and **yè** are the most common.

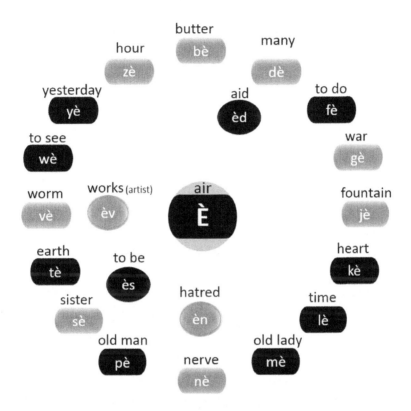

Li pa t di a ki lè L ap rive	He didn't know what time he's coming
Se ti sè M ni ye	She's my little sister
Moun yo pa travay tè ankò	The famers don't work the land anymore
Vwazen M nan gen bon kè	My neighbor has a good heart
Se pa fòt mwen, M pa t wè W	It isn't my fault, I didn't see you
Yè vè lè konsa …	Yesterday at this time …
Nap wè demen a menm lè a	We'll see you tomorrow at the same time
Li pa janm mande èd	She never asks for help
Kè L pa bat nòmal	Here heart doesn't beat regularly
Prezidan an prèke kòmanse on gè	The president is on the verge of starting a war

Two-Letter Words – È

kreyòl	english
èd	aid
èn	hatred
ès	is, east
èv	works (artist), charity
bè	butter
dè	many
fè	to do, to make, fact iron
gè	war
jè	spray, water fountain
kè	heart
lè	time, when
mè	old lady, sea, num
nè	nerves
pè	father, old man, peace, pair
sè	sister, nun
tè	earth, dirt
wè	to see
yè	yesterday
zè	time, hour

Konvèsasyon at the airport

A passenger at the airport (**ayewopò**) walks over to the ticket (**tikè**) counter (**kontwa**) to find out if his flight is on time. The ticket agent checks (**tcheke**) him in, assigns a seat, and wishes the traveler a safe trip.

Good afternoon, miss	Bonjou, madam
Good afternoon, sir	Bonjou, mesye
Can I check in now?	M ka tcheke kounyè a?
Or is it too early?	Ou byen ès ke L twò bonè?
Are you traveling today?	W ap vwayaje jodi a?
Yes I am traveling today	Wi, M ap vwayaje jodi a
What time is your flight?	A ki lè vòl ou a?
My flight is at 2 o'clock	Vòl mwen an a de zè
What is the flight number?	Ki nimewo vòl la?
The flight number is 1323	Nimewo vòl la se 1323
Do you have your passport?	Ou gen paspò W?
Yes, here it is	Wi, men ni
Are we on time?	Avyon an a lè?
Yes, we're boarding shortly	Wi, N ap anbake tout a lè
Here, sir, you are in seat 15A	Men, mesye, ou nan chèz 15A
Thank you very much	Mèsi bokou
You're welcome	Pa gen pwoblèm
Have a safe trip	Pase bon vwayaj
Thank you	Mèsi

WORD SEARCH

Although the accented letter **è** does not exist in English, it's a familiar sound, which is similar to the **e** in *let*.

B	F	C	E	N	X	È	P	S	E	R	K
C	H	A	S	È	E	F	L	A	V	I	A
S	È	L	U	O	D	R	I	L	L	A	N
L	E	S	K	C	Y	È	Z	A	S	È	S
È	K	M	H	È	L	T	Y	Y	È	N	È
T	U	A	È	A	K	È	È	È	S	T	N
È	L	A	T	N	Y	T	X	T	E	A	O
È	H	P	L	A	N	È	T	S	D	P	X
S	B	C	V	F	R	O	A	A	P	R	È
U	È	A	E	K	A	M	W	P	È	W	K
N	R	Y	E	P	È	B	S	I	R	È	N
T	G	S	P	N	L	R	È	N	O	B	P

AFTER	ALPHABET	AMEN
CANCER	COLD	DESERT
DISH	EARLY	HEAT
HUNTER	LETTER	PALACE
PASTOR	SINNER	PLANET
MANY	NONE	RESPECT
WEEK	TO BELIEVE	WORKER
SOME	HONOR	PARTNER
PAIN	SECRET	LATER

Lèt F

25-   THE LETTER F (LÈT F)

[ef]

F is one of the consonants, along with **l, m, n,** and **s** that sounds identical in both languages both in terms of pronouncing the letter itself and pronouncing it as part of a word.

"F" Word with Same Spelling and Meaning

Kreyòl	English
final *[fee-nahl]*	final

Sample Sentences – F

Kreyòl	English
Egazamen final yo ap kòmanse lòt semèn	The final exams will begin next week
Ekip Ameriken an rive nan final	The American team reached the finals
Ekip Fransè a chanpyon di mond	The French team is world champion
Eleksyon yo nan faz final yo	We reached the final phase of the elections
Ès ke ou konn rezilta final yo?	Do you know the final results?

"F" Words with Same Spelling but Different Meaning

Kreyòl	English
fad *[fahd]*	mild, faded
fame *[fah-mey]*	famous

fane *[fah-ney]*	to lose brightness, faded
fen *[fehN]*	thin, sharp (well dressed)
file *[fee-ley]*	to thread, sharpen, ask one out
fin *[feen]*	to finish
foul *[fool]*	crowd

Sample Sentences – F

Kreyòl	English
Manje a gen on gou fad	The food has a mild taste
Rad la gen on koulè fad	The dress has a faded color
File kouto a anvan	Sharpen the knife first
Doktè a fin fè operasyon an	The doctor is done with the surgery
Dantis la fin rache tout dan L yo	The dentist has removed all his teeth
Malad la fin refè nèt	The patient is completely healed
Li fin pale Kreyòl nèt	She is fluent in Creole
Li fin konn tout peyi a	She knows the entire country
Manje a poko fin kuit	The food is not ready yet
Politisyen yo fin detwi peyi a nèt	The politicians have completely destroyed the country
Mwen pa renmen foul	I don't like crowds
Yo met foul moun yo sou de ran	The crowd was lined up in two rows
Se premye fwa M wè on gwo foul moun konsa	This is the first time I see such a big crowd
Li fini apre tout moun	He finished after everyone
Gaz machin nan prèske fini	The car is almost out of gas
M mèt fin manje tout rès la, manman?	Can I finish eating the rest, Mommy?

The last sentence is quite useful for adoptive parents since it's a literal translation. A better one is: **Mom, can I eat the rest?** Here are a few others:

I am done showering Mommy, I'm going to get dressed
Mwen fin benyen manmi, mwen pwal aibye M

Honey, it's time you are done with your homework
Cheri li lè pou W fin fè devwa W

Aren't you finishing your meal honey?
Ou pap fin manje cheri?

Did you eat it all?
Ou fin manje tout?

It's time you finish eating so you can get ready for bed
Li lè pou W fin manje pou ou ka prepare W pou W al dòmi

Remember when asking questions, there are two possible forms: the sentence either begins with the subject, which is either a noun or an interrogative pronoun, or it begins with **ès ke**, which literally translates to "*is it,*" followed by the rest of the question.

Are you done getting dressed?
Ou fin met rad sou ou?
Or
Ès ke ou fin met rad sou ou?

"F" Words with Slightly Different Spelling

Kreyòl	English
fil *[feel]*	thread, string
filè *[fee-le]*	net
fini *[fee-nee]*	to finish
foule *[foo-ley]*	to stuff, or strain a muscle

Sample sentences – F

Kreyòl	English
Fil la pa ase fò	The thread is not strong enough
Yo kenbe pwason yo nan filè a	The fish are caught in the net

Filè a chire	The net is torn
Lè W fini wa fè M konnen	Let me know when you're done
Medikaman M yo prèske fini	I am almost out of medication
Mwen fini anvan tout moun	I'm done before everyone
Ou mèt fini rès la	You can finish the rest
Li foule L ak pye L	He stuffed it with his foot
Li foule mamit di ri a	He stuffed the can of rice
Li foule sachè a	He stuffed the bag full
Li foule ponyèt li	He strained his arm

26-   THE LETTER G (LÈT G)

G [*zhey*] shorten the sound. Do not pronounce the **y**.

G and *j* are tricky—the way you call out the letter and the sound by the two in a word are different in both languages. First, know that *g* always makes the hard *g* sound like in *give or go* and never the *j* sound as it does in English when it's followed by *e* like in *George*. Secondly, when you call out the letters themselves, the sounds are reversed. *G* is pronounced [*zhey*] (softer than English), while *j* is pronounced [*zhee*]. This is something that confuses English-learning French speakers all the time, and I am pretty sure you will face the same type of challenge when first starting out.

"G" Words with Same Spelling and Meaning

Kreyòl	English
global *[gloh-bahl]*	global
gratis *[grah-tees]*	gratis, free

Sample sentences – G

Kreyòl	English
Pi fò òganizasyon etranje yo se òganizasyon global	Most of the foreign organizations are global
Ban M on pri global	Give me a global price
Bidjè global peyi Ayiti pi piti pase nenpòt ki eta nan peyi Eta Zini	The total budget of Haiti is smaller than that of any of the states in the US

| Yo ba nou L gratis | They gave it to us for free |
| M mèt pran sa a gratis? | Can I take this one gratis? |

If you have been to Haiti or various underdeveloped countries around the world, I am sure you know that haggling is an art in some of those countries. If you do not know the language yet, it will be hard for you to haggle. Your interpreter or a native speaker accompanying you can certainly do it on your behalf. But if you feel adventurous and ready to do so, you can use the above sentence. You can also use the following sentences, which don't work on big ticket items but works very well on items like fruits. You may not need it, but it may turn out to be a lot of fun and the street vendors will certainly get a kick out of it.

| May I have this one as extra? | **M mèt pran sa a pou degi?** |
| Will you give me one gratis? | **És ke W ap ban M youn degi?** |

"G" Words with Same Spelling but Different Meaning

Kreyòl	English
gate *[gah-tey]*	spoil, rotten
gout *[goot]*	drop (of liquid)
grad *[grahd]*	rank, to elevate
grade *[grah-dey]*	rank
gran *[grahN]*	big, old
grate *[grah-tey]*	to scratch
grave *[grah-vey]*	to engrave, scratch
grip *[greep]*	cough (noun)
gripe *[gree-pey]*	head cold

Sample Sentences – G

Kreyòl	English
Pen an gate; voye L jete	The bread is bad; throw it away
Meteyo a te bay manti; pa t menm gen on gout la pli	The forecast was wrong; there wasn't even a single drop of rain
Kapitèn nan fèk pran on lòt grad	The captain's rank was recently elevated
Ki lè lame Eta Zini an ap gen on fanm ki rive nan grad general?	When will a lady in the American army reach the rank of general?
Se misye ki pi wo grade nan militè Ameriken an	This man is the highest ranking officer in the American military
Yo grave bag la avèk non koup ki marye a	They engraved the ring with the names of the married couple
Li blese grav	It's a serious wound
Se li ki pi gran nan tout ti moun yo	She's the oldest of all the kids
Misye se gran manjè; anvan W bat jye W, plat la ap vid	This guy eats a lot; before you blink, the plate will be empty
Di L piga li grate maling lan	Tell her not to scratch the wound
Li gen on grip ki pa janm kite L	He's had a cough he hasn't been able to shake off
Li gripe toujou?	Is she still coughing?

If you're a medical professional and feel adventurous, you can bypass your interpreter and use the last three sentences to ask a few direct questions to your patients. Below are some other questions and comments to a patient.

Kreyòl	English
Ès ke li grate W?	Is it itchy?
Piga ou grate L	Don't scratch it
Si W we L ap grate, se paske L prèske geri	If it's itchy, that means it's almost healed
Ou gripe toujou?	Are you still coughing?
Depi ki lè ou gripe?	How long have you been coughing?

Some cognates are more subtle than others and that is certainly the case for some of the examples listed below.

Kreyòl	English
gradye *[grah-dee-ey]*	to graduate
gradyasyon *[grah-dee-ah-see-ohN]*	graduation
gaz *[gahz]*	gas
grann *[grahN]*	grandmother
gras *[grahs]*	grace
gravye *[grah-vee-ey]*	gravel
grès *[gres]*	grease, fat

"G" Exception Words

The following *g* words have no connection to English. However, they're so common that I've listed them for your learning purpose. Pa egzanp, **gen**, the abbreviated form of **genyen** that translates to *"to have."*

Kreyòl	English
Gen (abbreviation) *[gehN]*	To Have (sound is very close to *gain*, with silent n)
Genyen (full) *[gehN-yehN]*	To Have
Grap *[grahp]*	Cluster, Bunch
Grenn *[gren]*	Grain, Pill
Gri *[gree]*	Grey, Drunk

Taking advantage of these fundamental words can make colorful sentences, such as the below phrase which uses the Kreyòl word **grap** instead of the English word *"grape."* Note the direct translation for grapes is *"rezen."*

He has a cluster of grapes that he's eating slowly, one grain at a time
Li gen on grap rezen ke L ap manje dousman grenn pa grenn

168

Sample Sentences – G

Kreyòl	English
Mwen pa gen okenn eksplikasyon pou M ba W	I don't have to give you any explanations
Mwen pa gen tan pou sa	I don't have time for that
Li pa gen pasyans pou ti moun yo	He doesn't have any patience with the kids
Li genyen nan bolèt de fwa	She won the lottery twice
Malad la grav; li pa gen anpil tan pou L viv	His condition is serious; he's not going to live long
Moun sa yo gran nèg	These people are rich
Nèg sa a toujou gri	This man is always drunk
Mwen renmen koulè gri sa a	I like this grey color
Di L pou L pran on grenn chak swa anvan L al dòmi	Tell her to take a pill every night before going to bed

The last sentence is another one that can allow medical professionals to speak directly with their patients. Giving this instruction directly would sound like the following:

Take a pill every night at bedtime

Pran on grenn chak swa anvan W al dòmi

Konvèsasyon

A patient visits the dentist because she's had a tooth ache for a while. She had the fortunate news that the tooth won't need to be extracted. A quick cleaning and some pills, and the patient is free to go home and scheduled to come back for a visit in two weeks.

What's wrong?	Kisa W genyen?
I don't feel well	Mwen pa santi M byen
What do you feel?	Kisa W santi?
I have a tooth ache	Mwen gen on dan k ap fè M mal
How long has it been hurting?	Depi ki lè L ap fè W mal?
It's been a long time	Sa gen lontan
Who brought you here?	Ki ès ki menenen W la a?
My grandmother	Grann mwen
Where is she?	Kote li?
She's outside, she's coming	Li deyò a, L ap vini
Sit on this chair	Chita sou chèz sa a
Open your mouth wide	Ouvè bouch ou laj
Let me take a look	Ban M wè
The tooth isn't that bad	Dan an pa twò grav
I won't have to pull it	M pap bezwen rache L
I'll just clean the infected area	M ap netwaye kote L enfekte a
I'll give you these pills	M ap ba W grenn say o
Thank you doctor	Mèsi doktè
Take one pill per day	Pran on grenn chak jou
Don't eat heavy food	Pa manje gwo manje
Don't chew anything like rice or meat	Piga W moulen diri ou byen viann
Come back to see me in two weeks	Retounen vin wè M nan de semen
Thank you very much doc	Mèsi anpil doc
I already feel better	M gen tan santi M miyò

27-   THE LETTER H (LÈT H)

[ahsh]

H always follows **c** to make up the sound **sh** like in *show,* not the **ch** sound. There are a few words with **tch** like in *match.* There actually aren't any Kreyòl words that begin with **h** with identical spelling to English, but I want to introcuce a few common words that begin with **ch**.

Common "CH" Words

Kreyòl	English
chache *[shah-shey]*	to search, look for
chèche *[she-shey]*	to search, look for
chanm *[shahNm]*	room
chagren *[shah-grehN]*	chagrin, grief
chaj *[shahzh]*	charge
chaje *[shah-zhey]*	to charge, load, fill
chak *[shahk]*	each
chalè *[shah-le]*	heat, warmth
chanje *[shahN-zhey]*	to change, switch, exchange
chanjman *[shahN-zh-mahN]*	change
cho *[show]*	hot, show
chè *[she]*	expensive
chèz *[she z]*	chair
mache *[mah-shey]*	to walk, market place
chwa *[shwah]*	choice
chita *[shee-tah]*	to sit down
chire *[shee-rey]*	to tear off

Sample sentences – H

Kreyòl	English
Elèv yo òganize on mach pou la pè	The students organized a march for peace
W ap vin chache M nan ayewopò?	Are you coming to get me at the airport?
W ap chèche pwoblèm?	Are you looking for problems?
Ki chaj yo pote kont gouvènè a?	What charge did they bring against the governor?
Yo chaje milèt la ak machandiz	They charged the mule with merchandise
Mwen pwomèt pou M pratike Kreyòl chak jou	I promise to practice Creole every day
Mwen cho	I am hot
Mwen santi chalè	I feel hot
M bezwen chanje lajan	I need to exchange some money
Se pa tout moun ki renmen chanjman	It's not everyone who likes change
Solèy la cho	The sun is hot
Bagay sa a twò chè	This thing is too expensive
Ba madanm nan chèz la	Give the chair to the lady
Chita bò kote M	Sit next to me
Ès ke ou pwal nan mache kounyè a?	Are you going to the marketplace now?
Al nan chanm ou	Go to your room
Ès ke ou ta renmen chanje chanm?	Would you like to switch to a different room?

Konvèsasyon nan Otèl la (I'm confident you can handle)

A guest checks in at the hotel and receives a warm welcome.

Bonjou, madmwazèl	Good morning, miss
Bonjou, mesye	Good morning, sir
M ka ede W?	Can I help you?
M gen rezèvasyon pou on chanm	I have a reservation for a room
Konben tan W ap pase?	How long are you staying?
Sis nuit	Six nights
M ka wè paspò W souple?	May I please see your passport?
Gen on rezèvasyon sou non W?	Is there a reservation under your name?
Kòman yo di non W?	How do you say your name?
Non M se Nancy	Nancy
M jwenn ni	I found it
Ou pito on gwo kabann ou byen de ti piti?	Do you prefer a king size bed or two queen beds?
Mwen pito on gwo kabann	I prefer king size
Ou prefere de kle ou byen on sèl	Do you prefer two keys or will one be enough?
On sèl la kont	One is enough
Men ni, madmwazèl	Here it is, Miss
Se premye fwa ou ret nan otèl la?	Is this your first time at the hotel?
Non, mwen rete isi a deja	No, I've stayed here before
Tanpri fè M konnen si gen on bagay ou bezwen	Please let me know if you need anything
Mwen la pou M sèvi W	I'm here to serve you
Mèsi	Thank you

28- THE LETTER I (LÈT I)

I
[ee]

I is never followed by a vowel as we often see in English. It's substituted with **y** when it would normally precede a vowel. Similar to English, i followed by **n** isn't a nasal as it is with **a, e,** and **o**. Pa egzanp, **la lin** means *"the moon"* and its pronounciation is similar to **fin**.

"I" Words with Slightly Different Spelling

Kreyòl	English
idantifye *[ee-dahN-tee-fee-ey]*	to identify
idantite *[ee-dahN-tee-tey]*	identity
idyo *[ee-dee-oh]*	idiot
idòl *[ee-dol]*	idol
idolatri *[ee-doh-lah-tree]*	idolatry
imaj *[ee-mahzh]*	image
imajine *[ee-mah-zhee-ney]*	to imagine
imajinasyon *[ee-mah-zhee-nah-see-ohN]*	imagination
inifye *[ee-nee-fee-ey]*	to unify
inik *[ee-neek]*	unique
inite *[ee-nee-tey]*	unity
inyon *[ee-nee-ohN]*	union
inisyasyon *[ehN-vah-zee-ohN]*	initiation
inisye *[ee-nee-see-ey]*	to initiate

Sample sentences – I

Kreyòl	English
Yo pa t ka idantifye ki ès ki responsab	They could not identify the responsible party
Ou ka montre M kat idantite W?	Can you show me your ID?
Piga ou janm rele ti moun nan idyo	You should never refer to the kid as idiot
Se premye pitit li; li trete L tankou on idòl	It's her first child; she treats her like an idol
Depi nan tan koloni yo te aboli idolatri	Idolatry was abolished since colonial times
Atis la rele Seesa, li genyen on stil inik	The artist's name is Seesa, she has a unique style
Nou gen plis fòs lè nou ini (lè N met tèt nou ansanm)	United, we are stronger
Inyon fè la fòs	United, we are strong
Inite se on bon premye pa	Unity is a good first step
Konbyen tan seremoni inisyasyon an ap dire?	How long is the initiation ceremony?
Se jodi a L ap Inisye	Today is the initiation day

One and Two-Letter Words – I

Many of the letters that sound like Kreyòl words end with **i**: **di, pi, si, ti**, and **vi**. There are 17 two-letter words in all that either begin or end with **i**, with the words in the black shapes being the most common.

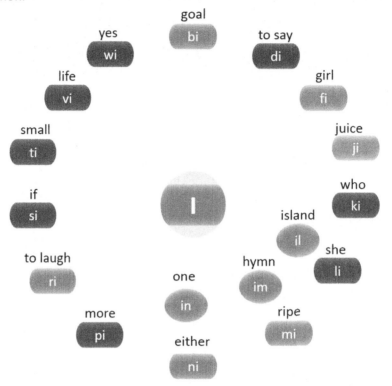

Ki ès ki pi gran?	Who's the oldest?
Li pa ni wo ni kout	She is neither tall nor short
Manje a pa ni cho ni frèt	The food is neither hot nor cold
Ès ke ji a byen glash?	Is the juice real cold?
Ki sa li di?	What did she say?
Ti moun yo ap aprann li	The kids are learning how to read
M ap kontan anpil, si W ri	I'll be very happy, if you laugh

Kreyòl	English
bi	goal
di	hard
fi	girl
il	island
im	hymn
in	one
ji	juice
ki	who
li	he, she, it, to read
mi	ripe, wall
ni	either, he, she, it
pi	more
ri	street, to laugh
si	if, sure
ti	small
vi	life
wi	yes

Konvèsasyon

A visitor engages a kid in a konvèsasyon wanting to know whether he goes to school and knows how to read. She ends up making arrangements to teach him how to read and buy him some books.

Do you know how to read?	Ès ke ou konn li?
No, I don't!	Non!
Where do you go to school?	Ki kote W al lekòl?
I don't go to school	Mwen pa al lekòl
Do you like school?	Ou renmen lekòl?
Yes I'd love to go to school	Wi M ta renmen al lekòl
What do you want to be when you grow up?	Kisa W ta renmen aprann lè W gran?
I'd like to be a pilot	M ta renmen vin pilòt
Do you like to read?	Ou renmen li?
I don't know how to read	Mwen pa konn li
But if I knew how to read, I'd love it	Men si M te konn li, mwen t ap renmen L
Would you like me to teach you?	Ès ke ou ta renmen M montre W?
Yes I'd like that	Wi M ta renmen sa
When will we start?	Ki lè N ap kòmanse?
Why don't we start now?	Pou kisa nou pa kòmanse kounyè a?
Will you buy me some books?	W ap achte liv pou mwen?
Yes, I'll buy you some books	Wi, M ap achte kèk pou ou
You think I can really become a pilot	Ou panse M ka vin on pilòt tout bon
Yes, of course you can	Wi, sètènman ou kapab
You should always believe that you can be whatever you want	Fò W toujou kwè ke W kapab vin nenpòt sa W vle

29-   THE LETTER J (LÈT J)

J
[*zhee*]

The sound that *j* makes in Kreyòl is softer than its English counterpart. It is the same sound made in "*déjà*," which is borrowed from French. It is a little challenging for English speakers but with practice, you'll nail it. A good way to practice and master the proper sound is to play with the difference between my name, Jacques, and the English version of it, Jack.

"J" Words with Same Spelling but Different Meaning

Kreyòl	English
jan *[zhahN]*	manner/way
jedi *[zhey-dee]*	thursday
jodi a *[zhoh-dee-ah]*	today

Sample sentences – J

Kreyòl	English
Ki jan?	How?
Ki jan ou rele? or ki non W	What's your name?
Ki jan ou ye?	How are you?
Ki jan ou vle l?	How do you want it?
Ki jan ou ta remen l?	How would you like it?
Ki jan ou vle pou M fè l?	How do you want me to do it?
M ap fè L jan W di M fè L la	I'll do it the way you told me
Jan Bon Dye renmen W	God loves you so much
K jou W ap vini?	When are you coming?

179

M ap vini Jedi	I am coming on Thursday
M te wè L Jedi pase	I saw him last Thursday
Jodi a se premye jou li pa fè la pli	Today is the first day it didn't rain
A la on bèl jounen jodi a	Today is such a beautiful day
Nan ki mwa nou ye?	Which month is this?
Nou nan mwa Janvye	We are in January

Konvèsasyon

Mom's waking her son up to get ready for school, but he's tired and wants to remain in bed for a few more minutes. Mom warns him that he needs to wake up so he doesn't miss the bus.

Li 8 è; li lè pou ou reveye	It's 8 o'clock, it's time to wake up
Pou kisa?	Why?
Li lè pou ou abiye W pou W al lekòl	It's time to get dressed for school
Dòmi nan jye M toujou	I'm still sleepy
M pa bezwen tande W	I don't care
Kite M fè on ti dòmi pou 30 minit ankò	Let me sleep for 30 more minutes
Pa gen sa pyès, leve kounyè a	No way, get up right now
Tanpri manman	Please mom
M pap jwe avè W, leve kounyè a	Not playing with you, wake up at once
M fatige	I'm tired
Ou te dwe vin dòmi pi bonè yè swa	You should have gone to sleep earlier last night
Manmi	But mom
Chak swa W al dòmi byen ta	Every night you go to bed very late
Tanpri kite M fè di minit an plis	Please let me sleep for ten more minutes
Tan an bèl epi solèy la klere deyò a	The weather is beautiful and it's sunny outside
OK M kontan	Good I'm happy
W ap pran plezi avè M?	Are you making fun of me?
M ap leve talè	I'll wake up in a few
Piga W pèdi bis la	You'd better not miss the bus

30- THE LETTER K (LÈT K)

K
[kah]

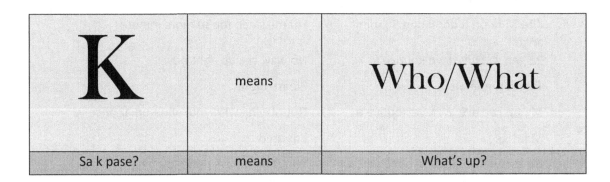

K	means	Who/What
Sa k pase?	means	What's up?

K is a very special letter because it's the most natural letter to represent the **k** sound. Since any given sound can be represented by only one letter in Kreyòl, all the other **k** sounds that you're used to (**c, ch, q**, and **qu**) are never used and are replaced by **k**. As a result, **k** is one of the most popular letters in Kreyòl.

It's also a single letter word, the abbreviated form of **ki** or **ke** which means *"who, what"* or "this, *that*." As mentioned earlier, the sound of the single letter word blends in with either the word that precedes or succeeds. They're never pronounced as you'd call out a letter of the alphabet. Pa egzanp, ***k ap*** is pronounced [*cap*] and ***sa k*** is pronounced [*sack*]. Remember, the pronunciation of **a** in *cap* is much like the sound made in *sack*.

He's the one who did it **Se li k fè L**

I taught her how to drive **Mwen k aprann ni kondi**

182

What's going on?	**Sa k ap fèt?**
Who's bringing it?	**Ki ès k ap pote L?**
What's up?	**Sa k pase?**

The last sentence is the first and most popular one typically taught in Kreyòl. The corresponding reply is:

Hanging in there	**N ap boule**

"K" Word with Same Spelling and Meaning

Kreyòl	**English**
klan *[klahN]*	group, gang

Sample sentences – K

Kreyòl	English
Ti mesye sa yo pa janm pran pa a klan bandi yo	These boys never mingle with the group of bandits
Pitit mwen pa nan pyès klan	My child does not belong to any gang

"K" Words with Same Spelling but Different Meanings

Kreyòl	English
kale *[kah-ley]*	to beat, to peel
kat *[kaht]*	four
kay *[kahy]*	house, home
kaye *[kah-yey]*	notebook, curdling milk
kim *[keem]*	suds, foam (soap)
kit *[keet]*	either
kite *[kee-tey]*	let, to leave

Sample Sentences – K

Kreyòl	English
Kale pòm nan pou pitit la	Peel the apple for the little child
Li bati on bèl kay pou papa L	She built a beautiful home for her dad
M pwal achte on lòt kaye	I'm going to buy another notebook
M pi renmen lèt kaye	I prefer curdling milk
Savon sa a fè anpil kim	This soap makes lots of suds
Kit se jodi a ou byen demen W ap peye kan mèm	Whether it's today or tomorrow, you'll pay either way
Pa kite sa rive	Don't let that happen
Ou ka kite M pale?	Will you let me speak?
Pa ale kite M	Don't go without me
L ap chagren si W kite L	He'll be sad if you leave him
Kit se kat ou se senk, li pa on gwo diferans	Whether it's four or five, it's not a big difference

Common "K" Words

Although the words below have very little to do with English, they're very common and so I've listed them for your use.

Kreyòl	English
ka *[kah]*	can, case
ke *[key]*	that, this, tail
kè *[ke]*	heart
ki *[kee]*	who, what
kis *[kiss]*	cyst
kopi *[koh-pee]*	copy
kòt *[kot]*	rib
kot, kote *[koh-tey]*	side, where
kritik *[kree-teek]*	critical
kritike *[kree-tee-key]*	to criticize

Sample Sentences – K

Kreyòl	English
Ès ke ou ka montre M pale Kreyòl?	Can you teach me how to speak Creole?
Ou ka aprann Kreyòl byen fasilman	You can learn Creole very easily
Ka W la grav	Your case is serious
Si W eseye, W ap ka fè L	If you try, you'll be able to do it
Ti bebe a kenbe ke chat la	The baby held the cat's tail
Se konsa ke yo toujou abiye	That's how they always dress
Doktè a di ke ou pa gen pwoblèm nan kè	The doctor said you don't have a heart problem
L ap fè W mal men fò W kenbe kè	It's going to hurt, but you have to be strong (literally: hold your heart)
Li pap janm bliye W; W ap toujou nan kè L	She'll never forget you; you'll always be in her heart
Ki sa W vle di pa sa?	What do you mean by that?
Ki ès ki fè sa a?	Who did that?
Ki ès ki ka di M on bagay an Anglè?	Who can tell me something in English?
Ki moun ki deja konn pale Kreyòl?	Who already knows how to speak Creole?
Doktè a ap fè L operasyon pou L retire kis la	The doctor will operate on her to remove the cyst

Cognates Starting with *Kon*

In English, there are 1,947 words starting with **con**. Many are cognates which means the same word exists in both English and Kreyòl with some minor differences in spelling and pronunciation. Some cognates aren't so obvious, but if you remember early on, you learned that the sound **k** is always written with a **k**. As a result, all those cognates begin with the letter **k** instead of **c**. Below is a subset.

Kreyòl	English
kominikasyon *[koh-mee-nee-kah-see-ohN}*	communication
kominike *[koh-mee-nee-key]*	to communicate
konfimasyon *[kohN-fee-mah-see-ohN]*	confirmation
konfime *[kohN-fee-mey]*	to confirm

konpare *[kohN-pah-rey]*	to compare
konpatriyòt *[kohN-pah-tree-ot]*	compatriot
konpoze *[kohN-poh-zey]*	to compose
konpozisyon *[kohN-poh-zee-see-ohN]*	composition
konseye *[kohN-sey-ee-ey]*	counselor
konsiderasyon *[kohN-see-dey-rah-see-ohN]*	consideration
konsidere *[kohN-see-dey-rey]*	to consider
konsil *[kohN-seel]*	consul
konstipasyon *[kohNs-tee-pah-see-ohN]*	constipation
konstipe *[kohNs-tee-pey]*	constipated
konstitisyon *[kohNs-tee-tee-see-ohN]*	constitution
kontak *[kohN-tahk]*	contact
kontakte *[kohN-tahk-tey]*	to contact
kontinye *[kohN-tee-nee-ey]*	to continue
kontra *[kohN-trah]*	contract
kontraktè *[kohN-trahk-te]*	contractor
kontwole *[kohN-troh-ley]*	to control
konvèsasyon *[kohN-ve-sah-see-ohN]*	conversation

Konvèsasyon

Two old friends meet and ask each other about their kids and their families.

Kreyòl	English
Kòman ou ye?	How are you?
Mwen an fòm	I am doing great
E ti moun yo; kòman yo ye?	How about the kids; how are they doing?
Yo pa pi mal	They are doing OK
Kòman fè M pa t wè W yè?	How come I didn't see you yesterday?
Mwen te genyen on ti pwoblèm	I had a small problem
Ki lè ti moun yo ap vini?	When are the kids coming?
Gen youn k ap vini demen	One of them is coming tomorrow
E lòt la; ki lè L ap vini?	How about the other one; when is she coming?
Li vini depi yè	She came yesterday
Ki lè M ap wè L?	When will I see her?
L ap vin wè W pi ta	She'll come see you later
M ap byen kontan wè L	I'll be happy to see her
M wè pa W yo tout tan, M pa bezwen mande pou yo	I see yours all the time, I don't have to ask about them
Wi, yo di M yo toujou pase wè W	Yeah, they tell me they always stop by to see yo
Se madanm nan mwen pa wò depi kòk tan; kòman L ye?	I haven't seen your wife in a long time, how is she doing?
Li trè byen	She's well

WORD SEARCH

K is a pretty popular letter in Kreyòl. It's used everywhere you hear the k sound. You should always be on the lookout for all the cognates that begin with **kon** in Kreyòl or **con** in English.

```
E   H   E   K   I   T   I   R   K   K   E   K
K   Y   C   M   P   I   K   E   O   O   K   K
A   O   N   A   I   U   Y   M   N   N   I   O
M   T   N   O   K   F   I   U   T   S   L   N
A   H   X   F   Y   N   N   E   A   I   P   P
K   O   N   D   I   S   Y   O   N   D   N   R
N   A   S   K   A   D   K   Q   K   E   O   A
D   E   E   Y   W   R   A   A   H   R   K   N
K   O   N   P   A   R   E   N   H   E   L   N
E   T   O   N   I   M   O   K   S   C   H   K
X   D   P   W   K   O   N   T   I   N   Y   E
E   L   O   W   T   N   O   K   E   K   A   P
```

ACCENT	ACTION	EVERY
CASH	TO COMMUNICATE	COMMUNITY
CONDITION	CONFIDENCE	TO CONFIRM
TO COMPARE	COMPLICATED	TO UNDERSTAND
TO CONSIDER	HAPPY	TO CONTINUE
TO CONTROL	CRAMP	TO CRITICIZE
TO MARK	TO PARK	SPICY

31- THE LETTER L (LÈT L)

L *[el]*

L	means	He/She
L ale	means	He/She goes

L is another single letter word. The abbreviated form of *li* which is the third singular pronoun. Like the letter *k*, *l* typically precedes the verbs that start with a vowel and is pronounced along with the verb as if it's a single word. Pa egzanp, *L ap* is pronounced "*lap*." To see it in action, *L ap tann* means "*he or she is waiting*." It's worth noting that there's no difference in gender, and whether it's a person or an object, we use the same pronoun, *li,* abbreviated as *L*.

"L" Words with Same Spelling and Meaning

Kreyòl	English
lave *[luh-vey]*	to lave, wash
legal *[ley-gahl]*	legal
liberal *[lee-bey-rahl]*	liberal
limit *[lee-meet]*	limit
long *[long]*	long

Long is one of the rare words that has the same spelling, same pronunciation, and same meaning in both languages.

Sample Sentences – L

Kreyòl	English
Y ap lave rad yo	They're washing the clothes
Li pa legal nan peyi a	It isn't legal in the country
Madanm sa a se on bon liberal	This lady is a true liberal
Ou ka manje sa W vle san limit	There's no limit to what you can eat
Li long anpil	It's very long
Li twò long; ou pap ka pote L nan avyon an	It's too long; you can't carry it on the plane
Li twò long pou machin nan	It's too long for the car

"L" Words with Same Spelling but Different Meaning

Kreyòl	English
lame *[lah-mey]*	army
lane *[lah-ney]*	the year
lase *[lah-sey]*	to lace (a shoe)
lateral *[lah-tey-rahl]*	lateral
lay *[ly]*	garlic

Below is another anagram in which the meanings of the words are identical. This is yet another great example of the closeness between Kreyòl and English when it comes to spelling.

Kreyòl	English
Lwa *[lwah]*	Law, Voodoo God

Sample Sentences – L

Kreyòl	English
Moun sa yo pa respekte lwa peyi a	These people don't respect the laws of the country
Si pa gen lwa, ap gen dezòd	Without laws, there will be disorder
Ès ke Ayisyen toujou kwè nan lwa?	Do Haitians still believe in Voodoo Gods?

"L" Words with Slightly Different Spelling

Kreyòl	Sounds like	Meaning
l ap	lap	he/she is + ing form
li sa	lisa	read it
se li sa	say lisa (y is silent)	that's him/her
lèt	let	letter, milk
lòt	lot (slight adjustment in o pronunciation)	other

Sample Sentences – L

Kreyòl	English
L ap pran leson Kreyòl nan men on bon pwofesè	She's taking Creole lessons from a great teacher
Moun ki ekri liv sa a bay leson Kreyòl si L enterese	If she's interested, the author of this book gives Creole lessons
Gen on egzamen literati demen	There's a literature exam tomorrow
Pase losyon an nan janm ou anvan W soti nan la ri a	Put the lotion on your legs before you go out on the streets

Cognates to Get Used to

A few chapters ago, we spoke of the differences in pronunciation between **g** and **j**. If you keep those differences and the substitution rules in mind, age and the other words listed below become fairly easy to memorize.

Kreyòl	English
laj *[lahzh]*	(the) age
lateralman [lah-tey-rahl-mahN]	laterally
leson *[ley-sohN]*	lesson
levye *[ley-vee-ey]*	lever
literalman *[lee-tey-rahl-mahN]*	literally
literati *[lee-tey-rah-tee]*	literature
losyon *[loh-see-ohN]*	lotion

Konvèsasyon

Konvèsasyon between a dad and his kid where the dad inquires about the kid's first day of school to find out that he likes his teacher, made two friends, and missed his him a whole lot.

How was your first day at school	Kòman premye jounen lekòl la te ye?
How do you like your teacher?	Ou renmen pwofesè W la?
I like her a lot	M renmen L anpil
Did you make any friends at school?	Ès ke ou fè okenn zanmi lekòl la?
Yes, I have two friends	Wi, M gen de zanmi
What are your friends' names?	Kòman zanmi W yo rele?
I don't know their names	Mwen pa konn non yo
Did you take a nap?	Ès ke ou te fè syès?
Dad, you know I don't like to sleep	Papa, ou konnen M pa renmen dòmi
You have to take naps; it's good for you	Fò W fè syès; li bon pou sante W
Do you have any homework?	Ès ke ou gen devwa?
No, we did all our work in class	Non, nou fè tout devwa nou nan klas la
Do you have anthing for me to sign?	Ou gen on bagay pou M siyen pou ou?
No Daddy	Non papa
I was sad all day Daddy	M te tris tout jounen an papi
Why were you sad?	Pou kisa ou te tris?
Because I missed you	Paske M te sonje W
I missed you too baby	M te sonje W tou cheri

32- THE LETTER M (LÈT M)

M [em]

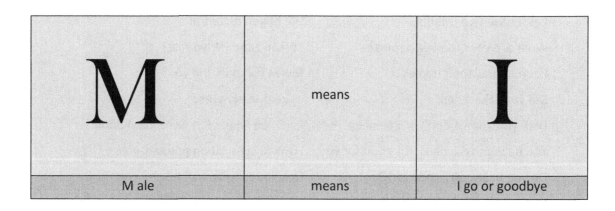

M	means	I
M ale	means	I go or goodbye

M is another single letter word. It's the abbreviated form of *mwen* which is the first-person singular pronoun. Just like *k* and *I*, *m* also typically precedes the verbs that start with a vowel and is pronounced along with the verb when used as a direct object. But as an indirect object, *M* succeedes the verb or it succeeds the noun as a possessive pronoun. Pa egzanp, *Li ban M* means "*He or she gave me*" and *M damou peyi M* means "*I love my country.*" In the last example, we see it as both a direct object and a possessive pronoun.

"M" Words with Same Spelling and Meaning

Kreyòl	English
mason *[mah-sohN]*	mason
match *[mahtch]*	match
memorize *[mey-moh-ree-zey]*	memorize

merit [mey-reet]	merit
metal [mey-tahl]	metal
moral [moh-rahl]	moral

Sample Sentences – M

Kreyòl	English
Misye se mason; li pa pè travay	He is a brick mason; he isn't afraid to work
Yo di fran mason gen on pakèt sekrè	People say the masons have a lot of secrets
Match la poko kòmanse	The match hasn't started yet
Li gen merit li; travay la pa t piti	He has some merit; the work wasn't trivial
A ki metal chenn nan fèt?	What metal is the chain made of?
Gen on pakèt moun ki pa gen moral	There are lots of people with no morals

"M" Words with Same Spelling but Different Meaning

Kreyòl	English
mache [mah-shey]	to walk, market
make [mah-key]	to mark
mare [mah-rey]	to tie down, fasten
mate [mah-tey]	to bounce (a ball)
Me [mey]	May (the month)
men [mehN]	hand, but, here
met [meyt] (abbreviated form of mete)	to put
motive [moh-tee-vey]	motivated
moto [moh-toh]	motorcycle
move [moh-vey]	bad, frown, upset

Sample Sentences – M

Kreyòl	English
Ès ke M ka al nan mache avè W?	Can I go to the marketplace with you?
M pwal fè on ti mache pou M ka pran on ti frechè	I'm going for a walk to get some fresh air
Li make L avèk on plim	She marked it with a pen

Mare bèf la nan lakou a	Tie the cow down in the backyard
Balon a pa gen van; se sa k fè li pa ka mate	The ball has no air; that's why it won't bounce
Mwen pwal Ayiti an Me	I'm going to Haiti in May
Majisyen an mare men L dèyè do L	The magician tied his hands behind his back
Se sa W di, men li pa kwè W	That's what you said, but he doesn't believe you
Men kote L abite	Here is where he lives
Met men W sou tab la	Put your hand on the table
Met men W dèyè do W	Put your hand behind your back
Li pa motive pou L fè anyen	He isn't motivated to do anything
Gen anpil moto ki fè taksi nan peyi a	There are lots of motorcycles that are used as taxis in the country
Li move; li pa vle pale avè W	He's upset; he doesn't want to speak with you
Se pi move bagay ou ka di	That's the worst you can say

"M" Words with Slightly Different Spelling

Kreyòl	R2R	Meaning
m al [mahl]	male	I go
mal [mahl]	male	bad, male
maladi [mah-lah-dee]	malady	malady, sickness
m ale [mah-ley]	male	I am going
malè [mah-le]	male	misfortune
marye [mah-ree-ey]	mary	married
mens [mehNs]	men's	thin
mèt [met]	met	can, owner, teacher
mete [mey-tey]	met	to put
mouvman [moov-mahN]	mouvement	mouvement
mov [mohv]	move	purple
mwen [mwehN]	men	I
mwen tou [mwehN-too]	me too	me too

Sample Sentences – M

Kreyòl	English
M ale	I'm going, Bye
M ale kite W	I'm leaving without you
M ale devan	I'm getting a head start
M ale pou kont mwen	I'm going by myself (alone)
Ou pap menm konn lè M ale	You won't even know when I leave
Se lè M fin ale li regrèt mwen	She missed me after I was gone
Priye pou li pou malè pa rive L	Pray for him so nothing bad happens to him
Gen on malè k rive yè	Yesterday something bad happened
Se premye fwa M wè on moun mens nan eta sa a	This is the first time I see such a thin person
Televizyon kounyè yo mens tankou on fèy papye	TVs nowadays are as thin as a sheet of paper
M ap dòmi	I am sleeping
Ki ès ki mèt kay sa a?	Who owns this house?
Ou mèt vin demen	You can come tomorrow
Mèt la poko rive	The teacher hasn't arrived yet
Mete L la a	Put it there
M konprann Kreyòl men M pako ka pale L	I understand Creole but I can't speak it yet
Mwen konprann Kreyòl men M pa ka pale L	I understand Creole but I can't speak it

In the previous example, note the use of both *mwen* and the abbreviated form, *M*. They are used interchangeably in both positions, but the sentence flows more naturally the way it's written above. Actually, the abbreviated form in both cases is also a good choice, but the full word "mwen" in both positions doesn't sound as smooth.

I am putting my hand on your back	**M ap met men M sou do W**
Can you pray with me?	**Ou ka priye avè M?**
You can leave without me	**Ou mèt ale kite M**
I put the food on the table	**Mwen mete manje a sou tab la**

197

Konvèsasyon

A young girl speaks passionately about her older sister. She truly loves her sister and expresses that love in this short konvèsasyon in which we learn both sisters' names and ages.

My name is Seesa	Mwen rele Sisa
How old are you?	Ki laj ou?
I'm seventeen years old	Mwen gen diset an
Do you have a brother or sister?	Ou gen on frè ou byen on sè?
I don't have a brother	Mwen pa gen frè
I have a sister	Mwen gen on sè
What's her name?	Ki non ni?
Her name is Nynie	Li rele Nayni
Are you older?	Se ou k pi gran?
No, my sis is older	Non, sè M nan pi gran
How old is she?	Ki laj li?
My sister is twenty-one	Sè M nan gen vente en lane
Do you all get along?	Ès ke nou antann nou?
Yes, she's my best friend	Wi, sè M nan se pi bon zanmi M
Do you like your sister a lot?	Ou renmen sè W la anpil?
Yes, and she loves me too	Wi, epi li renmen M tou
I can't wait to meet your sister	M pa ka tann pou M konn sè W la
I'll bring her over one day	M ap mennen L vin wè W on jou

33-   THE LETTER N (LÈT N)

N [*en*]

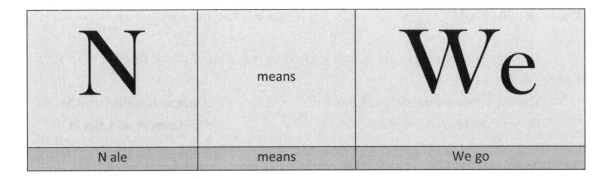

N	means	We
N ale	means	We go

N is the abbreviated form of both the first and second person plural **nou**. It's used as both the direct and indirect object just like the other pronouns.

"N" Words with Same Spelling and Meaning

Kreyòl	English
note *[noh-tey]*	to note, dictate

Sample Sentence – N

Kreyòl	English
Note byen ke se pa premye fwa li te fè sa	Note that it's not the first time he did that

"N" Words with the Same Spelling but Different Meanings

Kreyòl	English
nap *[nahp]*	tablecloth
nat *[naht]*	straw mat
niche *[nee-shey]*	to lick

Sample Sentences – N

Kreyòl	English
Met on nap sou chak tab	Put a tablecloth on each table
Bò isi a, se sou nat nou dòmi	Here, we sleep on straw mats
Chyen an niche pye M	The dog licked my foot

The following sentences are almost exclusively made up of words that are both Kreyòl and English:

The dog licked the back of my hand	**Chyen an niche do men M**
He put the bread on the plate	**Li met pen an nan plat la**

"N" Words with Slightly Different Spellings and Meanings

Kreyòl	R2R	Meaning
n ap *[nahp]*	nap	we are (ing form)
nich *[neesh]*	niche	nest (bird's)
nòt *[not]*	note	note (noun)
notè *[noh-te]*	note	notary public

Sample Sentences – N

Kreyòl	English
N ap vin chèche L	We'll come look for it
Zwazo yo fè nich nan mitan plant yo	The birds made their nests in between the plants
M ap pran nòt pou ou	I'll write down the notes for you
Fò W fè notè siyen L	You must get it signed by a notary public
Li pa ni cho ni fret	It's neither hot nor cold

Konvèsasyon

A traveler calls to say she and her sister are on their way, but they don't know when they'll reach their destination. The person she's talking to is patiently waiting and won't go to bed until they arrive.

Alo	Hello
Se ki ès?	Who is it?
Se mwen Sandra	It's me Sandra
Kote W ye?	Where are you?
Mwen sou wout	I'm on the way
Ou pou kont ou?	Are you alone?
Non, M avèk sè M nan Lynda	No, I'm with my sister Lynda
Nou gen lòt moun avèk nou?	Is there anyone else with you?
Non, nou de a sèlman	No, just us two
A ki lè N ap rive?	At what time will you arrive?
M pa konnen	I don't know
Kòman ou fè pa konnen?	How come you don't know?
M di W M pa konnen	I told you I don't know
N ap rele W lè N prèske rive	We'll call you when we get closer
OK, M ap tann nou rele M ankò	OK, I'll wait for you to call me back
Ou poko pwal dòmi?	You aren't going to bed yet, are you?
Non M ap ret tann nou	No I'll wait for you
Li pap pran N anpil tan	It isn't going to be much longer
Fè atansyon, pa kondi twò vit	Be careful, don't drive too fast

34-   THE LETTER O (LÈT O)

O [*oh*]

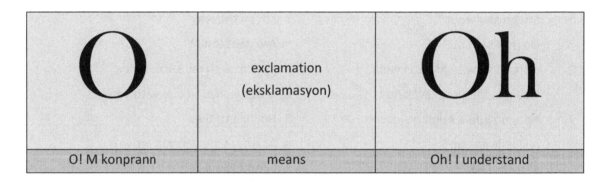

O	exclamation (eksklamasyon)	Oh
O! M konprann	means	Oh! I understand

The Kreyòl letter *o* is the exclamation "*oh*" in English. As stated earlier, in Kreyòl you should finish the ending sounds very abruptly.   However, the exclamations *ah* and *oh* are exceptions. The ending sound is emphasized depending on the impact or the severity of the information that is shared. Pa egzanp:

Oh, I understand   **O, mwen konprann**

Ah, don't do that, dear   **A, pa fè sa, ma chè**

"O" Words with Same Spelling and Meaning

Kreyòl	English
Oval *[oh-vahl]*	Oval

Sample Sentence – O

Kreyòl	English
Bòl la gen on fòm oval	The bowl has an oval shape
Boul la oval, li pa mate byen	The ball is oval, it doesn't bounce well

"O" Words with Same Spelling but Different Meaning

Kreyòl	English
On [ohN]	A, one
Out [oot]	August

Sample Sentences – O

Kreyòl	English
On bon jou M ap fè W sipriz	I'll surprise you one of these days
Premye pitit mwen an te fèt an Out	My first child was born in August
Ti moun yo ap tounen lekòl nan fen mwa Out la	The kids are returning to school at the end of August

One and Two-letter Words – O

There are 14 two-letter words that either begin or end with **O**. Amongst the most common are the pronouns **ou** and **yo**, the singular indefinite article **on**, **bo**, the equivalent of "*kiss*," and **to,** the equivalent of "*rate*" like in exchange rate.

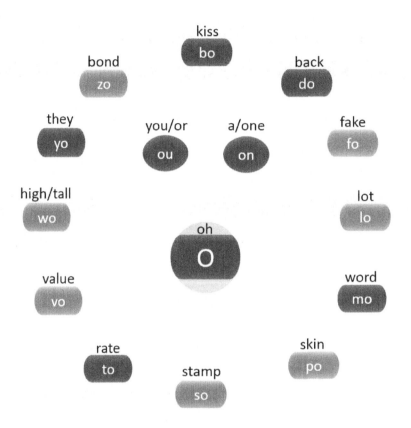

O, M pa t konn si W te vle L	Oh, I didn't know you wanted it
Se li k pi wo nan klas la	She's the tallest in the classroom
Ou gen doulè nan do?	Do you have back pain?
Pomad la bon pou egzema nan po	This ointment is good for skin eczema
On sèl mo li di	She only said one word
Li bo manman L sou bouch	He kissed his mom on the lips

Two-Letter Words – O

Kreyòl	English
on	a, one
ou	you, or
bo	kiss, handsome
do	back
fo	fake
lo	lot, prize
mo	word
po	skin, pitcher
so	seal, bucket (of water)
to	rate
vo	value
wo	high, tall
yo	they
zo	bond

35- THE LETTER Ò (LÈT Ò)

[o]

The accented vowel **ò** in Kreyòl sounds very similar to the short **o** in *other, mother,* and *sort.*

"Ò" Words with Similar Spelling but Different Meaning

Kreyòl	English
bòy *[boy]*	flour dough
lòt *[lot]*	other
nòt *[not]*	note
pilòt *[pee-lot]*	pilot
pòt *[pot]*	door
tò *[to]*	culpable
twò *[too-o]*	too, too much
sò *[so]*	friend (lady), fate

Common ò Words

Kreyòl	English
bò *[bo]*	side
bòks *[box]*	boxing
bòs *[boss]*	boss
efò, jefò *[ey-fo]*	effort
enfòme *[ehN-fo-mey]*	to inform

espò, spò *[spo]*	sport, exercise
fò *[fo]*	must, strong
fòk *[fock]*	must
kò *[ko]*	body, callus
kòmande *[ko-mahN-dey]*	to order, command
kòmanse *[ko-mahN-sey]*	to begin, start
kòmansman *[ko-mahNs-mahN]*	beginning
metòd *[mey-tod]*	method
mòso *[mo-soh]*	piece
pò *[po]*	port (shipment)
rapò *[rah-po]*	report
rekò *[rey-ko]*	record
rekòde *[rey-ko-dey]*	to record
sipò *[see-po]*	support

Sample Sentences – Ò

Kreyòl	English
Mande L ki bò li santi doulè a	Ask her where she feels the pain
M santi doulè a sou bò dwat la	I feel the pain on the right side
Fò W rive a lè	You must arrive on time
Nou te rive anvan fim nan kòmanse	We got there before the movie started
Sa a se sèlman kòmansman an	This is just the beginning
Fòk li ta di M sa nan figi M	He would have to tell me to my face
Ma vin ranje L on lòt jou	I'll come fix it another day
Fò W pentire pòt la	You must paint the door
Li fè anpil efò sè jou si	He tries very hard these days
M fè spò chak jou nan semèn nan	I exercise every day of the week
M fè spò chak jou (Bon Dye kreye)	I exercise every day (created by God)

One and Two-Letter Words – Ò

There are 10 two-letter words that either begin or end with ò. Amongst the most common are **bò** which means "side," **fò** which means *"smart, strong"* or *"must"* and **kò** which means *"body"* or *"callus."*

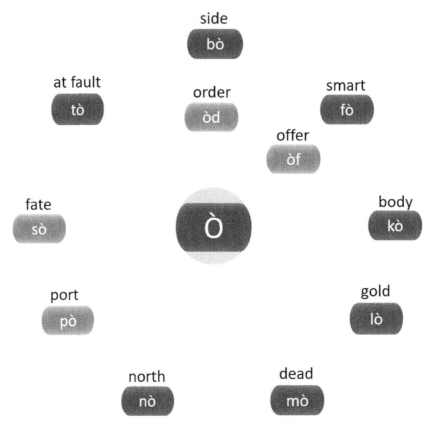

Ki bò W soti?	Where do you come from?
Mwen soti nan nò	I'm from the North
Pri lò monte sè jou si	The price of gold has risen these days
Malad la di tout kò L ap fè L mal	The patient said his entire body's aching
Li resi dakò ke L an tò	She finally admitted that she's at fault
Yo fè M on òf ke M pa t ka refize	They made me an offer I couldn't refuse
Li ba W on bèl òf pou kay la	She gave you a good offer for the house
Ti gason an fò anpil	This little boy is very smart
Yo rele yo pa òd alfabetik	They called them in alphabetical order

Kreyòl	English
bò	side
fò	strong
kò	body, callus
lò	gold
mò	dead person
nò	north
pò	port, pores
sò	girlfriend
tò	at fault
òd	order
òf	offer

WORD SEARCH

This word search puzzle is simple because most of the words are cognates. The only difference in a majority of the cases is the accent on the O in Kreyòl.

E	Ò	T	N	Ò	T	R	K	P	Ò	M	M
V	M	K	W	N	X	Ò	T	P	M	Ò	I
M	Ò	Ò	N	Ò	M	Ò	S	P	E	F	Y
D	K	P	F	A	N	E	T	A	T	I	Ò
N	E	S	N	N	U	V	H	Z	Ò	N	Ò
J	R	D	A	F	E	V	R	N	D	I	Y
O	E	K	P	O	S	I	P	Ò	T	E	E
A	E	F	K	U	T	Ò	L	I	P	W	D
B	L	T	Ò	T	Q	V	V	Q	Q	Z	M
Q	Ò	K	Ò	B	E	S	N	A	M	Ò	K
B	D	L	Ò	Ò	I	D	Ò	L	S	N	Q
Ò	P	A	R	L	B	H	Q	O	C	B	J

AGAIN	ALCOHOL	OUTSIDE
TO INFORM	SPORT	FOOTBALL
IDOL	UNIFORM	EFFORT
CANOE	TO ORDER	TO BEGIN
OTHER	METHOD	BETTER
PIECE	NOTE	OCTOBER
PILOT	REPORT	RECORD
TO SUPPORT	TOO MUCH	ZONE

36- THE LETTER P (LÈT P)

P

[*pey*] shorten the sound. Do not pronounce the **y**.

Ap and *pa* reverse each other in the sense that the former is the progressive form while the latter is the negative form. We combine the two to form the negative progressive form, *pap*. If you apply R2R to all three, I'm fairly certain you'll remember the following suggested rules. Think of Associated Press for **AP**, Physician Assistant for **PA**, and pap smear for *PaP*.

"P" Words with Same Spelling and Meaning

Kreyòl	English
papa *[pah-pah]*	papa, father
patch *[pahtch]*	patch
pin *[peen]*	pin
piston *[pees-tohN]*	piston, trumpet
plan *[plahN]*	plan
plant *[plahNt]*	plant
prepare *[prey-pah-rey]*	to prepare

Sample Sentences – P

Kreyòl	English
Li met on patch nan pantalon L	He put a patch on his pants
Machin nan gen pwoblèm piston	The car's piston has a problem
Misye se mizisyen; li jwe piston	This guy is a musician; he plays the trumpet
Li met on pin pou L sonje plas li	She added a pin to remember its place

211

Met plant la bò fenèt la	Put the plant next to the window
Achitèk la fin prepare plan bank la	The architect is done preparing the plan of the bank
M ap prepare M pou fèt la	I am getting ready for the party

"P" Words with Same Spelling but Different Meaning

Note that words like *pam, pan, and pat* are different from *pa M, pa N,* and *pa t* where the extra space separates the word *pa* from the single-letter words that follow *m,n,* and *t*.

Kreyòl	English
pale [*pah-ley*]	to speak, to talk
pan [*pahN*]	peacock
pans [*pahNss*]	belly
pant [*pahNt*]	slope
pap [*pahp*]	not + ing (progressive), won't
pare [*pah-rey*]	to be ready
pat [*paht*]	paste, dough
pate [*pah-tey*]	patty
pay [*pahy*]	straw, dust
pen [*pehN*]	bread
pete [*peh-tey*]	to fart, to blow up
pike [*pee-key*]	to poke, to stab, to dive, spicy, hot
pile [*pee-ley*]	to step on
plane [*plah-ney*]	to land, pawn
plat [*plaht*]	plate, dish
pot [*poht*]	to carry

Sample Sentences – P

Kreyòl	English
Yo pale san rete	They talk non-stop
Yo pap manje kounyè a	They aren't eating now
Nou pap vini san madanm nou	We aren't coming without our wives
Mwen pap rache dan an	I won't extract the tooth
Pan se on bèl zwazo, men nou pa genyen yo Ayiti	The peacock is a beautiful bird, but there is none in Haiti
Li gen on maladi nan pans	She has a disease in her belly
Machin nan pake sou on pant ki a pik	The car is parked on a steep slope
Li gen lontan depi L pare	She's been ready for a long time
La pli a pare depi maten	Since this morning rain is in the air
Se on pate sèlman M manje depi maten	I've only eaten a patty since this morning
Fòk ou kòmanse prepare pat pen an depi nan la vèy	You must start preparing the dough for the bread the night before
Ou toujou gen on bann pay nan cheve W	You hair is always dusty
Ti bebe a pete epi L ri	The baby farted and he started laughing
Manje a twò pike pou li	The food is too spicy for him
Li pile pye M epi li pa di M padon	She stepped on my foot and didn't say sorry
Li plane televizyon an paske lajan L te fini	He pawned the TV because he ran out of money
Li fèk fin lave plat yo; L ap repoze L	He just got done washing the plates; he's taking a break
L ap pot tout on sèl kou	He'll carry them all at once
Pot tout sa W ka pote	Carry all that you can

"P" Words with Slightly Different Spelling

Kreyòl	R2R	Meaning
pak *[pahk]*	pack	park
pake *[pah-key]*	pack	to park
pakè *[pah-ke]*	pack	pack

packèt [pah-ket]	pack	many, bunch
plante [plahN-tey]	plant	to plant
planèt [plah-net]	planet	planet
pa l [pahl]	pal	his/hers
pa M [pahm]	Pam	mine
pa N [pah-n]	pan	ours, yours (plural)
pa t [paht]	Pat	did not
pa w [pow]	paw	yours (singular)
pote [poh-tey]	pot	to carry
pòt [pot]	pot	door
pwojè [proh-zhe]	project	project, plan
pwojte [proh-zh-tey]	project	to project
pwoteksyon [proh-teyk-see-ohN]	protection	protection

Sample Sentences – P

Kreyòl	English
Li plante pye bwa tout a rebò kay la	She planted trees all around the house
Ou pale tankou on moun k ap viv sou on lòt planet	You speak like someone living on another planet
Pa L la pi gwo pase pa M nan	Hers is bigger than mine
Tout moun ta renemen gen pa N nan	Everyone would like to have ours
Li pa t konn si se te ou menm	She didn't know it was you
Li pa t konn si se te pa W la	She didn't know it was yours
Yo t ap pale de pa W la	They were talking about yours
Gen anpil pwojè ki pwal kòmanse nan koze Kreyòl la	A lot of Creole-related projects will be starting
Mwen poko gen pwojè pou M al Ayiti	I don't have any plans to go to Haıtı yet
L ap pote L sou tèt li	He'll carry it on his head

37-   THE LETTER Q (LÈT Q)

Q does not exist at all in the Kreyòl language because the sound made by *q* and *qu* is already taken up by *k*. As a result, *q* doesn't make the cut.

38-   THE LETTER R (LÈT R)

 [ehr]

There is a myth out there that *r* doesn't exist in Kreyòl. Although it's true that it doesn't play as prominent a role that it does in French, it's still used. There are many cases when it's omitted or replaced with *w*, which is more appropriate for the way we pronounce certain words. Pa egzanp, *route* is a cognate of *wout*, with the **r** being replaced by **w**. Whenever the *r* in English is followed by the letter *o*, it will often become a *w* in Kreyòl. With all other pronouns, r is unchanged. Pa egzanp, *ri* that means "to laugh" or "street," *ra*, which means "rare," or *reponn*, which means "to answer." **R** never precedes a consonant. It's simply left out and the English **o** is replaced with the accented **ò** to keep the short o sound: portable is **pòtab**, sort is **sòt**, sport is **spò**, and telephone is **telefòn**.

"R" Words with Same Spelling and Meaning

Kreyòl	English
rat *[raht]*	rat
respire *[rey-spee-rey]*	to respire
revoke *[rey-voh-key]*	to revoke, to fire
rich *[reesh]*	rich

Sample Sentences – R

Kreyòl	English
Rat la pi gwo pase on lapen	The rat is bigger than a rabbit
Nou mete pyèj pou rat yo	We put out some traps for the rats
Ti pitit la gen difikilte pou L respire	The little kid finds it difficult to breathe

Konsèy la pa rekòmande gouvènè an revoke pyès moun	The council has not recommended that the governor fire anyone
Fanmi moun sa yo se moun ki rich anpil	This family is very rich
Lè W rich sa pa vle di ou pa gen pwoblèm pa W	When you're rich that doesn't mean you don't have your own problems

"R" Words with Same Spelling but Different Meaning

Kreyòl	English
rabi [rah-bee]	stale
ran [rahN]	row, rank
rape [rah-pey]	to pull away abruptly
rate [rah-tey]	to miss
raze [rah-zey]	to shave
remake [reh-mah-key]	to see, notice
repo [rey-poh]	rest
rete [rey-tey]	to stay
retire [rey-tee-rey]	to remove

Sample Sentences – R

Kreyòl	English
Nan ki ran nou chita?	In which row are you sitting?
Yo raze tèt prizonye yo nan prizon an	They shave the prisoners' heads in the prison
Mwen remake ke chèf la pa fin twò byen	I notice that the chief is not well
Li rete nan kay la pou kont li	He stays in the house by himself
Li rape L nan men M	He abruptly pulled it away from me
Li pa janm rate on okazyon pou L di madanm li ke L renmen L	He never misses an occasion to tell his wife that he loves her
Rete tann mwen	Wait for me
Li rete san L pa di on mo	He remained quiet; he didn't say a word
Pou ki sa ou pa retire chapo a nan tèt ou?	Why don't you remove the hat from your head?
Li pa remake ke M retire tout bab yo	She didn't notice that I shaved off my beard

"R" Words with Slightly Different Spelling

Kreyòl	English
remak *[rey-mahk]*	remark
repoze *[rey-poh-zey]*	to rest
rès *[res]*	rest
responsab *[rehs-pohN-sahb]*	responsible

Sample Sentences – R

Kreyòl	English
Mòd remak sa yo pa fè madanm ou plezi	These types of remarks aren't pleasing to your wife
Rès sa L kite a pa anpil	The rest isn't that much
Ret tann yo	Wait for them
L ap ret tann ou anba a	She's waiting for you downstairs
M ap ret avè W jis tan anbilans la rive	I'll wait with you until the ambulance gets here
Ki ès ki responsab prensipal lopital la?	Who's the person in charge of the hospital?
Se pa responsablite L	It isn't his responsibility
Se li k responsab tout ti moun yo	He's responsible for all the kids

39-   THE LETTER S (LÈT S)

S [es]

Contrary to English where *c, s, sc,* and *ss* make the *s* sound, only one letter fulfills that function in Kreyòl, and that's **s**. As shown a few chapters back, there's only one letter that's sometimes doubled in Kreyòl and that's *n* since **ss** doesn't exist in Kreyòl. Therefore, words like *association*, pa egzanp, is spelled **asosyasyon**. As inherited from French, *ti* followed by a vowel also makes the **s** sound and is replaced by *s* as seen in the preceding example.

"S" Words with Same Spelling and Meaning

Kreyòl	English
salad *[sah-lahd]*	salad
satan *[sah-than]*	satan
solid *[soh-leed]*	solid
switch *[switch]*	switch

Sample Sentences – S

Kreyòl	English
Ban M prepare on ti salad pou ou	Let me prepare some salad for you
Vant mwen pa plen lè M manje salad	I'm not full when I eat salad
Tout moun konnnen salad bon pou la sante	Everyone knows salad is good for our health
Pon sa a pa solid	This bridge isn't sturdy
Li pa pi solid pase sa	It isn't that solid
Se solid, likid, ou byen vapè	It's solid, liquid or vapor
Li gen on switch pou ou limen L	There's a switch to turn it on

"S" Words with Same Spelling but Different Meaning

Kreyòl	English
sal *[sahl]*	dirty, room
sale *[sah-ley]*	salty
salon *[sah-lohN]*	salon
sen *[sehN]*	saint (male), breast
sent *[sehNt]*	saint (female)
sire *[see-rey]*	dirty
site *[see-tey]*	township, to cite
son *[sohN]*	sound
stat *[staht]* (the car, borrowed from English)	to start

Sample Sentences – S

Kreyòl	English
Rad yo sal; mwen pwal fè lesiv	The clothes are dirty; I'm going to wash them
Chanm nan sal; fòk M al netwaye l	The room is dirty; I'm going to have to clean it up
Ès ke ou ka site non twa ansyen prezidan Ayisyen?	Can you name three former Haitian presidents?
Nou pap janm bliye sa prezidan an di de peyi nou an	We'll never forget what the president said about our country
Lè M te jèn gason, chak maten papa M fè M stat machin nan	When I was a young boy, every morning my dad had me start the car
Machin nan pa stat	The car won't start

220

"S" Words with Slightly Different Spellings

In certain cases, R2R helps with memorization by creating the relationship that helps you remember vocabulary words or expressions. In other cases, it helps with pronunciation as almost all the words or expressions on the below table have similar pronunciation to the English words or expressions. For example, **Sa L** is pronounced similarly to Sal with the only nuance being that the vowel **a** is pronounced **ah**. The same rule applies to the next two expressions: **Sa M** and **Sa W**. For **sirèn**, you only need to remember that the vowel **i** is pronounuced **ee**; everything else is pronounced pretty much the same. There's also a slight difference in the **r** sound, but you'll be understood nonetheless. **Sistèm** is pronounced the same as its English counterpart *system*. The only word on this list that may present a challenge to pronounce is the last one, **sitiyasyon**, which is pronounced *[see-tee-yah-see-yohN]*

Kreyòl	R2R	English
sa L ...	sal	what he/she ...
sa M ...	sam	what i ...
sa W ...	saw	what you ...
sèl	sell	salt
sèt	set	seven
sirèn	siren	siren
sistèm	system	system
sitiyasyon	situation	situation

Konvèsasyon

The family is planning a trip and calling their relatives to announce their imminent visit. The host is very excited that the kids will be coming along and can't wait to see them.

When are you coming?	Ki lè W ap vini?
I'm coming on Saturday	M ap vini Samdi
Are the kids coming with you?	Ti moun yo pa vin avè W?
We haven't decided	Nou pako deside
But I think they're all coming	Men M kwè tout moun ap vini
Only one may not come	On sèl ki gen dwa pa vini
Who isn't coming?	Ki ès ki pap vini an?
Your favorite, Yvette	Moun ou pi renmen an, Yvette
She's starting school early	L ap kòmanse lekòl bonè
That's too bad, I'll miss her so much	Se byen domaj, M ap sonje L anpil
How many days are you staying	Konbyen jou N ap fè
We're staying seven days	N ap pase sèt jou
What, so many days?	Kisa tout jou sa yo?
The kids will be so happy	Ti moun you ap kontan anpil

40-   THE LETTER T (LÈT T)

T
[*tey*] shorten the sound. Do not pronounce the **y**.

T	represents	past tense
Yo t ale or yo te ale	means	They went

T, another single-letter word, is the abbreviated form of *te*, which marks the past tense. *Te* is also applied to past negatives like in "*didn't*." In the latter case, new speakers tend to use **te**, but native speakers always use the abbreviated form. Pa egzanp:

She left without me	**Li t ale kite M**
I didn't eat all	**Mwen pa t manje tout**

"T" Words with Same Spelling and Meaning

Kreyòl	English
tank *[tahNk]*	tank
timid *[tee-meed]*	timid
total *[toh-tahl]*	total

Sample Sentences – T

Kreyòl	English
Tank machin nan vid; fò N al fè gaz	The car is running on empty; we need to get gas
Jèn fi an timid, men se pa lè L ap chante	The young girl is shy, but not when she's singing
Ban M pri total tout sa M achete yo	Tell me the total price of all that I bought

"T" Words with Same Spelling but Different Meaning

Kreyòl	English
tab [tahb]	table
tan [tahN]	time, weather
tap [tahp]	slap
tape [tah-pey]	to hit, to spank
tip [teep]	type
tire [tee-rey]	to shoot
tout [toot]	all
ton [tohN]	sound, uncle
transpire [trans-pee-rey]	to sweat
trip [treep]	tripe
two [tu-oh]	too, too much

Sample Sentences – T

Kreyòl	English
Vye tab la gen on pye ki kase	One of the old table's legs is broken
Mwen pa gen tan kounyè a	I don't have time right now
Anpil politisyen tonbe nan pwoblèm pou tèt yo ba medam yo tap nan dèyè yo	Many politicians got in trouble because they slaped the ladies' rear ends
Madanm nan mechan; li tape ti bebe a sèlman paske L ap kriye	The lady is evil; she spanks the baby simply because he's crying
Al fè on ti te ten pou li	Go make some green tea for her

Ki tip de moun ou panse M ye?	What type of person do you think I am?
Menm kote polis yo rive a yo kòmanse tire	The police started shooting as soon as they got there
Mwen pa bezwen tout; M ap pran on sèl	I don't need all of them; I'll only take one
Si W ap kouri, W ap transpire kan mèm	If you're running, you will eventually sweat
Fò W retire trip kodenn nan	You have to remove the turkey's intestine
Ton Sebhastien renmen transpire	Uncle Sebhastien likes to sweat
Li pa janm twò ta pou N fè sa k bon	It's never too late to do what's right
Bon tan se nou, move tan se nou	We're there in good times as well as bad times

"T" Words with Slightly Different Spelling

Kreyòl	R2R	Meaning
talè *[tah-le]*	tale	later
tann *[tahN]*	tan	to wait
trafik *[trah-feek]*	traffic	traffic
transpòtasyon *[traNs-po-tah-see-ohN]*	transportation	transportation

Sample Sentences – T

Kreyòl	English
M ap fin fè L talè	I'll finish it later
Talè konsa L ap disparèt	Before you know it, she will vanish
Ou mèt tann mwen devan pòt legliz la	You can wait for me in front of the church
Ou twò gran pou W ap jwe jwèt sa yo	You are too old to play those types of games
Mwen bwè on kola chaq jou apre M fin manje	I drink a Cola every day after dinner
Madanm mwen pito bwè di ven anvan L manje, epi li bwè byè kon L fin manje	My wife prefers to drink wine before dinner and beer afterwards

41- THE LETTER U (LÈT U)

U is another one of those special letters that is always paired. It will either succeed *o* or precede *i*. When it comes to the cognates, wherever *u* is used as a stand-alone vowel, it's always substituted with *i*. As a result, there are no **u** words in Kreyòl; listed below are some cognates where **u** is replaced with **i**.

kreyòl	english
absoliman *[ahb-soh-lee-mahN]*	absolutely
distribisyon *[dees-tree-bee-see-ohN]*	distribution
evolisyon *[eh-voh-lee-see-ohN]*	evolution
inifòm *[ee-nee-fom]*	uniform
inik *[ee-neek]*	unique
inite *[ee-nee-tey]*	unity
inyon *[ee-nee-ohN]*	union
itilize *[ee-tee-lee-zey]*	to utilize
mizik *[mee-zeek]*	music
sitiyasyon *[see-tee-ah-see-ohN]*	situation

Common Words That Use U

Kreyòl	English
suit *[sweet]*	following
suiv *[sweev]*	to follow

Although **suit** is technically a Kreyòl word, it is exclusively used by those who know how to speak French. When speaking solely in Creole, the word **suiv**, which has the same root as **suit**, is used.

Sample Sentences – U

Kreyòl	English
Li fè anpil chalè nan mwa Out	It's very hot in August
Piga ou suiv li	Don't follow in his footsteps
M ap pran devan epi wa suiv mwen	I'll take the lead and you can follow me
L ap suiv nou pa pou pa	He's following us step by step

Words containing *ui* are rare. However, quite a few of them can come in handy and are listed here for you:

Kreyòl	English
uit *[weet]*	eight
kuit *[kweet]*	to cook
nuit *[nweet]*	night
luil *[lweel]*	oil

Sample Sentences – U

Kreyòl	English
Mwen ret uit jou pou M al Ayiti	There are eight days left before I go to Haiti
W ap kuit on ti manje pou nou?	Are you cooking for us?
Kòman ou te pase nuit la?	How was your night?
Mwen pwal achte luil pou M kuit manje a	I'm going to buy some oil to cook the food

Here are a few words containing the blend **ou**

Kreyòl	English
kou *[koo]*	neck, hit like in hitting someone
la bou *[lah-boo]*	mud
lou *[loo]*	heavy
nou *[noo]*	we, us

ou [oo]	you, or
sou [soo]	on
tou [too]	also, too
toujou [too-zhoo]	always
tout [toot]	all
twou [twoo]	hole

Sample Sentences – U

Kreyòl	English
Li sou medikaman pou maladi a	She's takin medication for her sickness
Machin nan kouvri a la bou	The car is covered with blood
Malad la gen on pwoblèm kou rèd	The patient has a stiff neck
Tanpri kouvri M, mwen santi fredi	Please cover me, I'm cold

Lèt V

42- THE LETTER V (LÈT V)

V [*vey*] shorten the sound. Do not pronounce the **y**.

Vini sounds just like Vinny and it means "to come." If you travel to a Kreyòl speaking country or communicate with anyone from those countries, you'll have plenty of opportunities to use this word. The more you put it to use, the more natural its usage will become. Getting comfortable with terms or sentences like the ones below will take you one step closer to fluency.

"V" Words with Same Spelling and Meaning

Kreyòl	English
veteran *[vey-tey-rahN]*	veteran
vital *[vee-tahl]*	vital
vitamin *[vee-tah-meen]*	vitamin
vote *[voh-tey]*	to vote

Sample Sentences – V

Kreyòl	English
Madanm sa a se veteran nan lame Ameriken	This lady is a veteran in the American army
Kominikasyon se on eleman vital nan nenpòt ki relasyon	Communication is a vital element of any relationship
Syantis yo di ke vitamin D enpòtan pou moun ki pa pran ase solèy	The scientists say vitamin D is important for people who don't get enough exposure to the sun
Se a ki laj moun Ayiti ka vote?	What is the voting age requirement in Haiti?

"V" Words with Same Spelling but Different Meaning

Kreyòl	English
vale *[vah-ley]*	to swallow
van *[vahn]*	wind, fart
vide *[vee-dey]*	to pour

Sample Sentences – V

Kreyòl	English
Gen anpil moun ki pa renmen vale grenn	There are many people who don't like to swallow pills
Li vale manje a san L pa kraze L	He swallowed the food without chewing
Chak aprè midi gen on ti van frèt	Every afternoon, there's a cool breeze
Lè gen anpil van konsa, mwen toujou pè pou pa gen siklòn	Whenever there's so much wind, I am always worried about hurricanes
Vide tout nan gode a	Pour it all in the cup
Soup la gou; ou mèt vide tout rès la nan bòl mwen an	The soup is tasty; you can pour the rest in my bowl
Vide aspirin nan nan men M	Pour the aspirin into my hand
Li vale on bon valè aspirin	She swallowed a good amount of aspirin

"V" Words with Slightly Different Spelling

Kreyòl	R2R	Meaning
valè *[vah-le]*	vale	value
vann *[vahn]*	van	to sell
vant *[vahnt]*	van	belly
vante *[vahn-tey]*	van	to boast
varyete *[vah-ree-ey-tey]*	variety	variety
ven *[vehn]*	vein	twenty, wine
venn *[vehn]*	vein	vein
verifye *[veh-ree-fee-ey]*	verify	to verify
verite *[veh-ree-tey]*	verity	truth
vòt *[vot]*	vote	vote (noun)

Sample Sentences – V

Kreyòl	English
Bagay sa a pa gen valè	This thing has no value
M si ke M ap vann tout pi ta	I'm sure I'll sell all later
Vant mwen poko plen; M ka manje toujou	I'm not full yet; I can eat some more
Chèf la renmen vante; se sa L fè pi byen	The chief loves to boast; that's what he does best
M gen ven tan epi M pa janm travay nan vi M	I'm twenty years old, and I've never worked a day in my life
Enfimyè a ap chache venn nan pou L ka met sewòm nan	The nurse is looking for the vein to put the IV
Legliz la vid; tout moun al lakay yo	The church is empty; everyone has gone home
Mache vit, la pli a pwal kòmanse tonbe	Walk fast, as it will start raining soon
Ou fèt pou ou kwè ke vòt ou a ap fè anpil diferans	You must believe that your vote will make a major difference

Konvèsasyon

It's quite common for strangers (**etranje**) to strike a konvèsasyon with you. A konvèsasyon between a tourist (**touris**) travelling locally (**lokal**) by bus (**bis**) and a friendly bystander may go as follows:

M ka ede W, madanm?	Can I help you, ma'am?
Wi M ap tann otobis la	Yes, I'm waiting for the bus
Ki bò W pwale?	Where are you going?
Mwen pwal Sen Mak	I'm going to Saint-Marc
Ou gen lontan W ap tann?	Have you been waiting long?
Wi, M gen on bon ti tan M ap tann	Yes, I've been waiting for a little while
Pran on ti pasyans; Y ap vini on lòt moman	Be patient; it won't be long before they get here
A ki lè bis la abitye rive?	What time do they usually arrive?
Yo pa gen on lè fiks; se pa menm jan a peyi etranje	They don't have a fixed time; it's not like the foreign countries
Kisa ou vle di?	What do you mean?
Pa gen anyen ki ijan konsa isi	There's no such urgency here
Pran pasyans, Y ap rive lè yo rive	Just be patient, they'll get there when they can
Ou renmen sa konsa?	Do you like it that way?
Se pa on kesyon de renmen; se konsa nou fonksyone	It's not whether or not I like it; that's the way we do things
M pa abitye a sa	I'm not used to that
Bò isi a nou pa ba tèt nou twòp strès pou bagay konsa	Over here we don't stress too much over stuff like that
M on ti jan dakò avè W wi	I tend to agree with you somewhat

Konvèsasyon an Kontinye

A, men bis la ap vini; ou wè sa M te di W la?	**Ah, here comes the bus; you see, what did I told you?**
Bon vwayaj	**Have a safe trip**
Ou pap vwayaje tou? M panse ou t ap tann bis la tou wi	Aren't you travelling? I thought you were also waiting on the bus
Non, M pa pwal okenn kote; M sèlman t ap fè konvèsasyon	Nope, I'm not going anywhere; I was just having a conversation with you
Mèsi pou tèt ou te kenbe M konpayi (on ti souri)	Thanks for keeping me company (chuckle)
Pa gen pwoblèm, fè bon vwayaj	No problem, have a safe trip

43- THE LETTER W (LÈT W)

[*doo-bley-vey*]

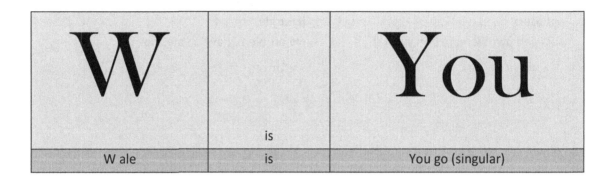

W	is	You
W ale	is	You go (singular)

W is quite common and is used in a similar fashion to English. Most of the time it precedes *a* or *o*. For those who speak French, *wa* is a substitute for *oi* and *roi* in French and is pronounced just like *wa* in water. In front of *o, r* is typically subsitituted with *w*.

Kreyòl	French	English
lwa	loi	law
twa	trois	three
wa	roi	king
vwazen	voisin	neighbor
pwofesè	professeur	professor
pwononse	prononcer	to pronounce
pwoteje	protéger	to protect

The spelling of proper names like Ronald, Robert, and Rose don't change to satisfy the above rule. However, *rose* is spelled **woz**. *Romance* is spelled **womans**, which is yet another cognate, but not an obvious one because of the substitution of **r** with **w**. It's important to learn to recognize that those cognates that aren't so obvious. The more you recognize them, the more your vocabulary will improve.

"W" Words with Same Spelling but Different Meaning

Kreyòl	English
won *[wohN]*	round
wont *[wohNt]*	ashamed
woman *[woh-mahN]*	romantic novel
womans *[woh-mahNss]*	romance
women *[woh-mehN]*	roman

Sample Sentences – W

Kreyòl	English
Balon an manke van; se sa k fè li pa sanble L won	There is not enough air in the ball; that's why it doesn't look round
Mwen wont pou manti M te ba W la	I'm ashamed for having lied to you
Mwen renmen li woman anpil	I truly enjoy reading romantic novels
Gen on womans anba anba ant de moun sa yo	There's a covert romance between these two people
Maten an mwen li women chapit 1, vèsè 5 e 6	This morning, I read Romans chapter 1, verse 5 and 6

"W" Words with Slightly Different Spelling than English

Kreyòl	English
wè *[we]*	to see
wi *[wee]*	yes
wikenn *[wee-ken]*	weekend

Sample Sentences – W

Kreyòl	English
Ès ke ou wè san linèt yo?	Do you see without the glasses?
Konbyen dwèt ou wè?	How many fingers do you see?
Wi, mwen konprann tout sa W di	Yes, I understand everything you say
Wi, li fè M mal anpil	Yes, it hurts a lot
M ap kite lopital la wikenn k ap vini an	I'm leaving the hospital next weekend
L al benyen nan lan mè chak wikenn	She goes to the beach every weekend

44-   THE LETTER X (LÈT X)

 *(written KS or GZ)*

Just like *q*, *x* does not exist at all in the Kreyòl language. If you pronounce any word with an *x* slowly, you'll hear two distinct sounds: *ks* or *gz* *like in exam (**egzamen**), and sexy (**seksi**).* Those are the two blends that are used to represent *x*.

Note that *ks* is also the substitute for *ct* when in English, the letters that follow are *i* followed by a vowel. Pa egzanp, *action* is a classic cognate and is spelled *aksyon* in Kreyòl.

Similarly, *cc* followed by *i* or *e* also sounds similar to *x* and is also represented by *ks*. Pa egzanp, *accent* (*aksan*). In this last egzanp, not only do we see the *ks* substitute, but we also see *en* substituted with *an*.

There obviously are no **x** words that are spelled the same in both languages because *x* will always be substituted with one of the aforementioned blends **gz** or **ks**. However, there are plenty of cognates, and if you keep in mind the various substitutes you already know, it becomes quite easy to recogize them. *Egzanp*, which I'm certain you've been using since you started reading this book, is ironically one of those cognates.

"X" Words with Slightly Different Spelling

Kreyòl	English
aksyon *[ahk-see-ohn]*	action
ekspè *[eyk-spe]*	expert
eksplikasyon *[eyk-splee-kah-see-ohN]*	explanation
eksplike *[eyk-splee-key]*	to explain
eksplwatasyon *[eyk-splwah-tah-see-ohN]*	exploitation
eksplwate *[eyk-splwa-tey]*	to exploit
ekspò *[eyk-spo]*	export
ekspòte *[eyk-spo-tey]*	to export
ekspoze *[eyk-spoh-zey]*	to expose
ekspozisyon *[eyk-spoh-zee-see-ohN]*	exposition
egzèsis *[eyg-ze-seess]*	exercise
egzijans *[eyg-zee-zhahNs]*	demands, requirements
egzije *[eyg-zee-zhey]*	to demand, require
maksi *[mahk-see]*	maxi
maksimòm [mahk-see-mom]	maximum
okside *[ohk-see-dey]*	to oxidate
oksijèn *[ohk-see-jen]*	oxygen
saksofòn *[sahk-soh-fon]*	saxophone
sèks *[seks]*	sex
seksi *[seyk-see]*	sexy
taksi *[tahk-see]*	taxi
toksik *[tohk-seek]*	toxic

Sample Sentences – X

Kreyòl	English
Li se on ekspè nan Kreyòl	He's a Creole expert
Mwen pwal nan ekspozisyon pou atis yo	I'm going to the exposition for the artists
Fò W fè egzèsis pou ou ka ret an sante	You have to exercise if you want to remain healthy

Se pa tout Ayisyen ki kwè nan fè edikasyon sou sèks	Not all Haitians believe in sexual education
Mòd aksyon sa yo pap ede nan anyen	These types of actions are not useful at all
Ou pa bezwen pè; M ap ba W pwoteksyon	No need to fear; I'll protect you
Menm si ou gen on aksan pa pè fè convèsasyon	Even if you have a strong accent don't shy away from engaging in conversations
Kondi pi dousman pou W pa fè aksidan	Drive slower so you don't get into an accident
Li di l pi seksi pase tout moun	She said she's sexier than everyone
Misye metrize saksofòn nan	She's mastered the saxophone
N ap ret tann taksi depi lontan	We've been waiting for the taxi for long
Ou ka pran taksi nan ayewopò Pòtoprens la byen fasilman	You can easily catch a cab at the airport in Port-au-Prince
Li manke oksijèn li gen difikilte pou L respire	She is short on oxygen, she has difficulty breathing

45-   THE LETTER Y (LÈT Y)

[*ee-greg*]

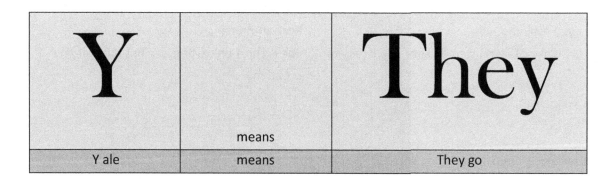

Y	means	They
Y ale	means	They go

Y is very common in Kreyòl. It's yet another characteristic of Kreyòl that brings it closer to English than French. One of the first grammatical rules that is important to know is that two vowels typically don't follow each other except in two cases: **ou** and **ui**. Wherever you'd normally see two vowels back to back in English, the Kreyòl version will have a **y** inserted between them to make the [*ill*] sound. The word **Kreyòl** is the best egzanp where the **e** and **o** follow each other in all the other laguages (e.g. Créole in French and Creole in English) but not in **Kreyòl**. Another case is where **i** is replaced by **y** when i is followed by another vowel. This is evident in the various words ending with **tion, sion, tial**, and **tiel**, where **ti** or **si** is substituted by **sy**.

Common Y Words

While the following words have very little connection with English, they are useful to know.

Kreyòl	English
byen *[bee-ehn]*	good
dèyè *[de-ye]*	back, behind

genyen [gehN-yehN]	to have
mannyè, manyè[mahN-nee-e]	manner
pye [pee-ey]	foot, feet
salye [sah-lee-ey]	to salute, say hi
vwayaj [vwa-ee-ahzh]	trip
vyann [vee-ahn]	meat
vye [vee-ey]	old
ya [yah]	they will
ye [yey]	to be
yè [ye]	yesterday
yo [yoh]	they
yon [yohn]	one
youn [yoon]	only one
travay [trah-vah y]	work
travayè [trah-vah-ye]	worker
senyen [sehN-yehN]	to bleed
penyen [pehN-yehN]	to comb
ponyen [pohN-yehN]	to grab
ponyèt [pohN-yet]	arm
ponpye [pohN-pee-yeh]	fire engine
manyen [mahN-yehN]	to touch, to handle
panye [pah -nee-yeh]	basket
popilasyon [poh-pee-lah-see-yohN]	population
yanm [yahNm]	yam
mayo [mah-yoh]	t-shirt
sitiyasyon [see-tee-yah-see-yohN]	situation
pasyon [pah-see-yohN]	passion
pasyone [pah-see-yoh-ney]	passionate
misyon [mee-see-yohN]	mission
relasyon [rey-lah-see-yohN]	relation
emosyon [ey-moh-see-yohN]	emotion
bagay [bah-gah y]	thing

Sample Sentences – Y

Kreyòl	English
Ban M youn	Give me one
Youn nan yo gate	One of them is bad
Kòman kouzen nou yo ye?	How are your cousins?
Yè se premye jou M te santi M byen	Yesterday was the first day I felt good
Kote mesye yo bay?	Where did the guys go?
M ap fè on ti vwayaj lòt semèn	I'm travelling next week
M pwal nan misyon ak legliz mwen an	I'm going on a mission trip with my church
Si W pasyone de Kreyòl, W ap aprann ni byen vit	If you're passionate about Creole, you'll learn it quickly
Fò W gen bon relasyon avèk pitit ou	You must have a healthy relationship with your kid
Ki kote M ka achte on mayo ki ekri "Onè Respè"?	Where can I buy a t-shirt that says "Onè Respè" (Honor Respect)?
Si M manyen W la, ès ke L fè W mal?	If I touch you here, does it hurt?
Ponyèt la pa kase, se anfle L anfle	Your arm isn't broken, it's just swollen
M ap oblije fè W operasyon nan ponyèt la	I'll have to operate on your arm
Anpil moun pèdi ponyèt yo nan tranbleman tè 12 Janvye 2010 la	Many people lost their arms during the earthquake of January 12, 2010
Se on bagay M pa ka eksplike	It's something I can't explain
Ayisyen rele tout bagay bagay LOL	Haitians refer to everything as a thing LOL
Ki bagay?	What?
Se on bèl bagay	It's a beautiful thing
Se on bèl bagay lè de moun damou	It's a beautiful thing when two people are in love

Konvèsasyon

Two old friends haven't seen each other for a long time. They run into each other and inquire about the wife, kids, and their travel plans.

Kòman W ye zanmi M?	How are you my friend?
Mwen an fòm; e moun yo?	I'm doing well; how is everybody doing?
Yo pa pi mal	They're not bad
E ti misye yo; gen kèk tan mwen pa wè yo	How about your boys; it's been a while since I've seen them
Tout moun la Y ap degaje yo	Everyone is well; they're hanging in there
Sa fè lontan nou pa wè	It's been a long time since we've seen each other
Ban M nouvèl madanm nan non?	How is your wife doing?
Li toujou ap travay kòm enfimyè?	Is she still working as a nurse?
Wi, L ap pran pansyon nan twa zan	Yes, she's retiring in three years
Ou pa vwayaje ankò?	Don't you travel anymore?
Gen plizyè ane mwen pa pati, men M pwal Mayami ane sa a	It's been many years since I've traveled, but I'm going to Miami this year
Pa bliye di Sasou mwen sonje L	Don't forget to tell Sasou I miss her
M ale wi	I'll get on my way
OK, babay, na wè	OK, bye, see you later

46-   THE LETTER Z (LÈT Z)

Z [zed]

In English, the sound **z** may be represented by an **s** or a **z**. In Kreyòl, it's always a **z**. There are many cognates between the two languages that are easily recognizable with the only difference being that the **s** substituted with a **z**.

In addition, you will often see cases in which words begin with the letter **z** because of a feature inherited from French called *"liaison"*. This is when the final consonant of a word that is usually silent is voiced when the following word begins with a vowel. To clarify, the plural form of *"the"* in French is *"les,"* with a silent **s**, but when it is followed *"anges"* (angels), the ending **s** in *"les"* is pronounced as **s**. *"Les anges"* sounds like [*le-zahN-zh*], and because the article moves after the noun in Kreyòl, we end up with **zanj yo** for "the angels."

"Z" Words with Same Spelling and Meaning:

Kreyòl	English
demoralize [dey-moh-rah-lee-zey]	demoralize
finalize [fee-nah-lee-zey]	finalize
legalize [ley-gah-lee-zey]	legalize
minimize [mee-nee-mee-zey]	minimize
mobilize [moh-bee-lee-zey]	mobilize
polarize [poh-rah-lee-zey]	polarize
zip [zeep]	zip

"Z" Words with Slightly Different Spelling

Kreyòl	English
analize *[ah-nah-lee-zey]*	to analyze
kolonize *[koh-loh-nee-zey]*	to colonize
itilize *[ee-tee-lee-zey]*	to utilize
pozisyon *[poh-zee-see-ohN]*	position
reyalize *[rey-ah-lee-zey]*	to realize
rezon *[rey-zohN]*	reason
sezon *[sey-zohN]*	season
sivilize *[see-vee-lee-zey]*	civilized
trayizon *[trah-ee-zohN]*	treason
zam *[zahm]*	arms
zanj *[zahN-zh]*	angels
zanno *[zahN-noh]*	earings
zansèt *[zahN-set]*	ancesters
ze *[zey]*	eggs
zen *[zehN]*	gossip
zo *[zoh]*	bone
zòn *[zon]*	zone
zong *[zohNg]*	nails (finger or toe)
zonyon *[zohN-yohN]*	onions
zoranj *[zoh-rahN-zh]*	oranges
zòrèy *[zo-rey]*	ears
zòrye *[zo-ree-ey]*	pillow
zòtèy *[zo-tey]*	toe
zuit *[zweet]*	oysters, crumbs
zwazo *[zwuh-zoh]*	birds

Note the various examples like *reason, poison, treason,* and *position* where the **z** sound is represented by **s** in English, but **z** in Kreyòl. If you're writing letters or emails to someone who speaks Creole, I suggest that you get in the habit of writing some of these words in Creole.

Sample Sentences – Z

Kreyòl	English
Moun sa yo toujou ap fè zen	These people are always gossiping
Zipe zip ou anvan W pran la ri a	Zip your zipper before you take to the street
Se on gwo zak ki ka mete W an danje	This is a significant act that can place you in a dangerous situation
Li fè enfeksyon nan zòrèy la	Her ear is infected
Zòtèy la dejwente	The toe is dislocated
Nou fyè de travay zansèt nou yo te fè	We're proud of our ancestors' accomplishments

Common Z Words

Kreyòl	English
dezipe *[dey-zee-pey]*	to unzip
repoze *[rey-poh-zey]*	to repose, to rest
zafè *[zah-fe]*	affairs, things, no matter
zam *[zahm]*	guns, weapons
zewo *[zey-roh]*	zero
zipe *[zee-pey]*	to zip up
zonbi *[zohN-bee]*	zombie

Sample Sentences – Z

Kreyòl	English
Sa a se zafè pa W; Mwen pap mele ladann	This is your business; I am not getting involved
Gen de kote o Zeta Zini moun mache nan la ri a zam yo	There are places in the United States where people carry their weapons on the streets
Zipe valiz la anvan ou soti	Zip up the bag before going out
Dezipe sak la pou M wè sa k gen ladan L	Unzip the bag for me to see what's in it
Mwen pa ka di W anyen; mwen pa moun nan zòn nan	I can't tell you anything; I don't live around here
M pa kwè nan koze zonbi a mwen menm	I don't believe in the rumors about zombies

Some cognates containing *s* make a [*zh*] sound in English, but the Kreyòl substitute is still *z*. These are harder to recognize, but because they are so common, I felt compelled to include in your vocabulary.

Kreyòl	English
mezi *[mey-zee]*	measure
mezire *[mey-zee-rey]*	to measure
plezi *[pley-zee]*	pleasure
trezò *[trey-zo]*	treasure

Sample Sentences – Z

Kreyòl	English
Voye mezi yo ban M, menm kote W rive a	Send me the measurements, as soon as you arrive
Vin mezire rad la pou ou wè si L bon pou ou	Come try on the dress to see if it fits
Dantis la te pran mezi anvan L fè danti a	The dentist took the measurements before making the denture
Apantè a te mezire tè a	The surveyor measured the lot
Se on plezi pou M fè konesans ou	It's a pleasure to meet you
Mwen pran anpil plezi lè Mwen Ayiti	I have a lot of fun when I'm in Haiti
Anvan yo te kite Haiti, kolon yo te piye trezò peyi a	Before they left Haiti, the colonizers pillaged the country's treasures

Konvèsasyon

A neighbor arrives in New York and tells her neighbor whom she hasn't seen in a while about her trip. She goes on to share that she's tired from having very little sleep because she stayed up late packing the night before the trip.

Kòman vwayaj la te ye vwazen?	How was your trip neighbour?
Li pat twò mal non	It wasn't bad
Kounyè a ou fatige?	You are tired now, aren't you?
Anpil	A lot
Depi yè swa M pa dòmi	I haven't slept since last night
Sa k fè sa?	How come?
Li te byen ta Mwen t ap ranje malèt mwen	I was packing my suitcase until it was very late
Maten an mwen leve byen bonè pou M al ayewopò	I woke up real early this morning to go to the airport
M wè ou pèdi vwa W	I see you lost your voice
M si tèlman fatige	Yeah, I am so tired
Ti moun yo kontan wè W?	Are the kids happy to see you?
O wi, ou konnen, yo gen lontan yo pa wè M	Oh, yeah, you know, it's been a long time since they've seen me
Konbyen tan W ap pase avè nou fwa sa a?	How long are you staying with us this time?
M ap pase de mwa	I'm staying two months
A, W ap fè on bon ti tan	Ah, you're staying a while
M kontan wè W anpil, vwazen	I'm very happy to see you, neighbor
Al repoze W; N ap gen kont tan pou N pale	Go get some rest; we'll have plenty of time to catch up

Part IV

The Nasals & Blends

47- THE BLEND AN (AN)

$\mathrm{An}_{[ahN]}$

The nasal sounds can be a bit difficult for English speakers. Using what I call the "Jean Rule," can help make sure you pronounce it correctly. Jean is one of the most common Haitian first names for males. You might have met someone named Jean, Jean-Claude, Jean-Jacques, Jean-Philippe, Jean-Marie, or Jean-Baptiste. But if you have been calling those guys Jean pronounced *Jeen,* you've been doing yourself a huge disservice. I'd also add that the guys with Jean in their names have failed you as well by not teaching you the proper way to pronounce their names. Although this may sound like political correctness, that's not the intention. By learning the proper way to pronounce the name Jean, you learn two of the most difficult Kreyòl sounds for English speakers to master: the softness of *j*, pronounced [*zh*] and the nasal ***an,*** pronounced [ahN] like in *avant-garde*. Instead of *Jeen,* it's more like [*zhahN*] with a silent -n at the end.

Take the time to practice pronouncing this very useful sound because it is very common in Kreyòl and quite different from anything you're used to in English. It will take some getting used to, but with a little practice you'll get it.

Two of my favorite words in terms of similarities between English and Creole are ***a*** and ***an,*** primarily because they are both synonymous, and they play almost the exact same role in both languages.

A and **An** are indefinite articles in English that are placed before the noun, but in Kreyòl they're definite articles placed after the noun. Egzanp:

Manje a	The food
Avyon an	The airplane

"An" Words with Same Spelling and Meaning

Kreyòl	English
plan [plahN]	plan
plant [plahNt]	plant

"An" Words with Same Spelling but Different Meaning

Kreyòl	English
an [ahN]	the, age
ant [ahNt]	between
ban [bahN]	to give, let, bench
dan [dahN]	tooth
pan [pahN]	peacock
tan [tahN]	time, weather
van [vahN]	wind
woman [woh-mahN]	novel

Sample Sentences – AN

Kreyòl	English
Dan an ap fè M mal	My tooth is hurting
Ant de madanm sa yo, ki ès ki manman L?	Between those two ladies, who's the mom?
Mwen pa gen anpil tan	I don't have a lot of time
Tan an pa bon menm	The weather is not good at all
Van an ap vante fò, epi li fè frèt	It's very windy, and it's cold
Ti fi sa a renmen li woman	This little girl likes reading romantic novels

Common "An" Words

Kreyòl	English
angaje [ahN-gah-zhey]	to angage
angajman [ahN-gahzh-mahN]	engagement
anvan, avan [ah-vahN]	before
anvi [ahN-vee]	need

251

ansyen *[ahN-see-ehN]*	ancient, old
anyen *[ahN-yehN]*	nothing
danje *[dahN-zhey]*	danger
dantis *[dahN-tees]*	dentist
devan *[dey-vahN]*	in front
fanm *[fahNm]*	woman
fann *[fahn]*	to split
frekan *[frey-kahN]*	someone who's fresh
gan *[ghahN]*	glove
jan *[zhahN]*	way, manner
Janvye *[zhahN-vee-ey]*	January
kann *[kahn]*	sugar cane
kòman *[ko-mahN]*	how
lang *[lahNg]*	language, tongue
manke *[mahN-key]*	missing
mannken *[mahn-kehN]*	mannequin, model
manyen *[mahN-ee-ehN]*	to touch, handle
medikaman *[mey-dee-kah-mahN]*	medicine
moman *[moh-mahN]*	moment
nan *[nahN]*	in
pann *[pahn]*	to hang
pant *[pahNt]*	slope
pantan *[pahN-tahN]*	to astound, startle
pantalon *[pahN-tah-lohN]*	pants
pran *[prahN]*	to take
san *[sahN]*	without, blood, 100
sann *[sahn]*	ash
tann *[tahn]*	to wait
vanjans *[vahN-zhahNs]*	vangeance
vanje *[vahN-zhey]*	to avange
vann *[vahn]*	to sell
vant *[vahNt]*	belly
vantilatè *[vahN-tee-lah-te]*	fan (air)

There are cases where *n* is sandwiched between two vowels and does not make the nasal sound. In those cases, its sound goes with the vowel that succeeds it rather than the one that precedes it. For example, ***ane*** is pronounced *[ahney]* and means *year*. Below are additional examples:

"An" Words that Aren't Nasals

Kreyòl	English
ane *[ah-ney]*	year
depane *[dey-pah-ney]*	to repair
fanatik *[fah-nah-teek]*	fanatic, fan
plane *[plah-ney]*	to pound

Although it's rare, there are some cases where **á** has an accent. Those are the cases in which **a** is followed by **n** and the sound isn't a nasal. The accent is used to differentiate as shown in examples like **pan** which means *peacock* and **pán** that is used to describe a machine that doesn't function properly.

Kreyòl	English
bekán *[bey-kah-n]*	bicycle
pán *[pah-n]*	broken down (car)
plán *[plah-n]*	pound shop

Konvèsasyon

Two friends talk about their evening plans and their preference for restaurants versus noisy night clubs.

Where is your wife?	Kote madanm ou?
She's resting upstairs	L ap repoze L an wo a
Are you guys staying in tonight?	N ap ret lakay nou a swè a?
We aren't planning to go out	Nou pa gen plan pou N sòti
You guys never want to go out	Nou pa janm renemen sòti
How come?	Sa k fè sa?
We like peace and quiet	Nou renmen la pè
We don't like lots of noise	Nou pa renmen briganday
Sometimes it's good to have a bit of fun	Gen de lè li bon pou ou amize W
I agree with that	M dakò a sa
But we don't like the night clubs	Men nou pa renmen al nan diskotèk
I certainly understand	Sètènman M konprann
We prefer restaurants when we go out	Nou pito al nan restoran lè N soti
One day to live my friend	De jou a viv patnè
But you also have to be careful to not over do it	Men fò W fè atansyon tou pou ou pa fè twòp

48-   THE BLEND EN (EN)

 [ehN]

This blend is probably the most confusing aspect of writing Kreyòl for native speakers who are fluent in French. *En* sounds like *en* in *men* or *pen* with the difference being that *n* is silent in Kreyòl. A sound you're familiar with that's closer to the one made in Creole is *sent* in which **n** is silent. It's not exactly the same but it's close. The only time **n** is pronounced is when it is doubled. Pa egzanp, **pen** is *bread* and the **n** is silent. However, in **penn** like in **la penn,** means *chagrin* or *pain*. In this case, the second **n** is pronounced.

At the end of a French movie, you may sometimes see *FIN*, which means *the end* in English. In Kreyòl, however, it is written as **FEN**, but natives who are educated in French tend to write it in French: **FIN** unless they're formally taught the correct way to write it in Kreyòl.

"En" Words with Same Spelling but Different Meanings

Kreyòl	English
men *[mehN]*	hand
pen *[pehN]*	bread
ten *[tehN]*	leaf (tea)
zen *[zehN]*	gossip, trouble

255

Sample Sentences – EN

Kreyòl	English
Ban M kenbe men W	Let me hold your hand
Li kenbe men M fò	He held my hand with a firm grip
Se pen sèlman L ka achte	She can only afford to buy bread
Pen enpòtan anpil nan rejim Ayisyen	Bread is very important in the diet of the Haitians
Mwen pa vle nan zen	I don't want to get in trouble

Cognates with "En"

The blends **in** or **im** followed by **m** or **p** like in *impossible* or *imbecile,* are substituted by **en** as seen in the examples below.

Kreyòl	English
Endyen *[EhN-dee-ehN]*	Indian
endividyèl *[EhN-dee-vee-dee-el]*	individual
engra *[EhN-grah]*	ingrate
enpòtan *[EhN-po-tahN]*	important
enpòtans *[EhN-po-tahNs]*	importance
enspire *[EhNs-pee-rey]*	inspired
enspirasyon *[EhNs-pee-rah-see-ohN]*	inspiration
enstitisyon *[EhNs-tee-tee-see-ohN]*	institution
enstriksyon *[EhNs-treek-see-ohN]*	instruction
enstriman *[EhNs-tree-mahN]*	instrument

Common "En" Words

Kreyòl	English
benyen *[behN-yehN]*	to bathe
bezwen *[bey-zwehN]*	need
byen *[bee-ehN]*	well
enfim *[ehN-feem]*	lame

256

enfimyè [ehN-fee-mee-e]	nurse
enkapab [ehN-kah-pahb]	incapable
fen [fehN]	thin
genyen, gen [gehN]	to have
kenbe [kehN-bey]	to hold
konbyen [kohN-bee-ehN]	how much, how many
kraponnen [krah-pohN-nehN]	to chicken out
maten [mah-tehN]	morning
mennen [mehN-nehN]	to bring, lead
monnen [mohN-nehN]	change (money)
nen [nehN]	nose
penyen [pehN-yehN]	to comb
plen [plehN]	full
plenyen [plehN-yehN]	to wine
pwen [pwehN]	dot, period
pwente [pwehN-tey]	to point
retounen, tounen [rey-too-nehN]	to return, come back
sen [sehN]	saint, breast
senyen [sehN-yehN]	to bleed
swen [swehN]	care (noun)
swenyaj [swehN-ee-ahzh]	care (noun)
tenten [tehN-tehN]	crap

49- THE BLEND IN (IN)

In doesn't have a nasal sound in Kreyòl and sounds similar to English. For those of you who are familiar with French, it's important to not confuse words like **fin** and **vin**.

The Kreyòl **fin** isn't a noun as it is in French. It's a verb and the abbreviated form of **fini**, which means "*to finish.*" *End* in Kreyòl isn't **fin**, it's **fen**.

Vin isn't a noun, nor does it mean "*wine*" like it does in French. The pronunciation is different as well. In Kreyòl, it's the abbreviated form of **vini**, which means "*to come.*" **Vini** is pronounced exactly like the Italian name, Vinny. *Wine* in Kreyòl isn't **vin**, it's **ven** or **di ven**.

"In" Words with Same Spelling

Kreyòl	English
fin [*feen*]	to finish
pin [*peen*]	pin

Sample Sentences – In

Kreyòl	English
Mwen fin fè tout	I'm done with all of them
Li fin di sa L t ap di a	He said what he had to say
Li pèdi ti pin nan	He lost the small pin
Yo pa vle fin fè L	They don't want to finish doing it

Common "In" Words

Kreyòl	English
Ginen [*gee-nehN*]	Guinea
inisyal [*ee-nee-see-yahl*]	initial
inisyasyon [*ee-nee-syah-syohN*]	initiation
inisye [*ee-nee-see-ya*]	to initiate
initil [*ee-nee-teel*]	worthless
min [*meen*]	frown, mine (metal)
minit [*mee-neet*]	minute
minui [*mee-nwee*]	midnight
pini [*pee-nee*]	to punish
pinisyon [*pee-nee-see-ohN*]	punishment
vini, vin [*veen*]	to come

Addition Sentences – In

Kreyòl	English
Ti madanm sa a toujou gen de min nan fwon L	This little lady always looks angry
Nou pa kwè nan bay ti moun pinisyon	We don't believe in punishing our kids
Li minui, al nan kabann nou	It's midnight, go to bed
N ap rive nan on lòt minit	We'll arrive in one more minute
Ayisyen se nèg Ginen	Haitians are from Guinée
Se Ginen nou ye	We're from Guinée

Konvèsasyon

A driver stops at a gas station and takes advantage of the opportunity to have her tires and oil checked. She also asks for the traffic conditions and directions to go into town.

Konbyen gaz ou bezwen?	How much gaz do you need?
Ou mèt plen L si L vou plè	Please fill it up
Ki kalite pou M mete?	What kind of gaz?
Ou mèt met sa k pi bon mache a	You can put the cheapest
Tanpri tcheke lwil avèk kawotchou yo tou	Please check the oil and tires too
Tout bagay an fòm wi	Everything is okay
Mwen pwal la vil, ou ka ban M direksyon?	I'm going in town, can you give me directions?
Lè M fin met gaz la M ap di W ki jan pou ou ale	When I'm done with the gaz, I'll tell you how to get there
Ès ke gen anpil trafik?	Is there lots of traffic?
Toujou gen trafik isi	There's always lots of traffic here
Men a lè sa a li pap anpil	But at this time it won't be that bad
Trafik la pi rèd nan maten	Traffic is heavier in the morning
Konbyen tan li ka pran pou M rive la vil?	How long will it take to drive into town?
Li ka pran ven minit konsa	It might take around twenty minutes
Lè W ap tounen li ka pran plis tan	It might take longer on the way back
Pou kisa W di sa?	Why do you say that?
Paske se lè tout moun ap sot travay	Because that's when everyone's leaving work
M konprann, sa fè sans	I understand, that makes sense

50- THE BLEND ON (ON)

Similar to *en*, *on* makes a similar sound in both English and Kreyòl with the difference being that the ending -*n* is silent in Kreyòl.

"On" Words with Same Spelling and Meaning

In terms of similarities between the two languages, some words have the same spelling and meaning, but not the same pronunciation, while others may be pronounced the same but have completely different meanings and spellings. A third category of words are spelled the same, but their meanings and pronunciations are completely different. Well, *long* is one of a handful of words that share the same spelling, pronunciation, and meaning. Another one is *soup*.

Kreyòl	English
Long *[long]*	Long

"On" Words with Same Spellings but Different Meanings

Kreyòl	English
don [*dohN*]	gift
non [*nohN*]	no, name
on [*ohN*]	a, an, one
son [*sohN*]	sound
ton [*tohN*]	rhythm
won [*wohN*]	round

Common "On" Words

Kreyòl	English
bon [*bohN*]	good
bonbon [*bohN-bohN*]	cookie
konpare [*kohN-pah-rey*]	to compare
konparezon [*kohN-pah-rey-zohN*]	comparison
konprann [*kohN-prahn*]	to understand
fon [*fohN*]	deep
fwon [*fwohN*]	forehead
kon [*kohN*]	like
konn [*kohn*]	to know
konnen [*kohN-nehN*]	to know
mon [*mohN*]	my
pon [*pohN*]	bridge
sonj [*sohN-zh*]	dream
sonje [*sohN-zhey*]	to remember

When *n* ends a word or is followed by a consonant, we get the nasal sound. However, when it's followed by a vowel, it's paired with that vowel in terms of sound. Therefore, the following examples are not nasals:

Kreyòl	English
bonè [*boh-ne*]	early, hat
bonèt [boh-net]	hat (binny type)
onè [*oh-ne*]	honor, knock knock
onèt [oh-net]	honest
sonèt [*soh-net*]	bell

Sample Sentences – ON

Kreyòl	English
Met on bout pen nan plat la	Put a piece of bread on the plate
M ap repete L on sèl fwa	I'll only repeat it once
On sèl jou ki rete	There is only one day left
Non, M pap ka di W	Nope, I can't tell you
Ki non W?	What's your name?
Aparèy la gen bon son	The stereo sounds good
Sonje sa W t ap di a	Remember what you had to say
Pa gen anpil politisyen ki onèt tankou misye	There aren't many politiciens who are ash honest as this man
Ou gen dwa rich nan dènye degre, ou pa ka achte bonè	No matter how rich you are, you can't buy happiness
Nèg "facebook" la rich anpil, men mèt "Amazon" nan pi rich toujou	The facebook guy is very rich, but the founder of Amazon is even richer
Se mesye ki fè konpayi teknoloji yo ki pi rich nan moman an	Nowadays the founders of the tech companies are the richest

51-   THE BLEND OU (OU)

The blend **ou** sounds like **ou** in *you* **and** is also a word that has two different meanings. The pronoun *you* also means *or*. Some additional notables are **tou**, which means *too* or *also*, and **tout**, which means *all* and **moun** is *people*. **Jou** is *day*, **bon jou** is *good day* or *good morning*, **fou** is *crazy*, **pou** is *for*, **gou** is *tasty,* and **sou** means *on* or *inebriated*.

"Ou" Words with Same Spelling

Kreyòl	English
bout [*boot*]	piece
foul [*full*]	crowd
gout [*goot*]	drop of liquid
soup [*soup*]	soup

Common "Ou" Words

Kreyòl	English
bon jou[*bohN-zhoo*]	good morning
la bou [*lah-boo*]	mud
boul [*bull*]	ball
bous [*boos*]	wallet
bouyon [*boo-yohN*]	stew
double [*doo-bley*]	to double
dous [*doos*]	sweet

dousman [*doos-mahN]*	slow, quiet, docile
douz [*dues*]	twelve
fou [*foo*]	crazy
fout [*foot*]	damn
gou [*goo*]	taste, tasty
jou [*zhoo*]	day
jounen [*zhoo-nehN*]	day
joure [*zhoo-rey*]	to curse
kou [*koo*]	neck, hit
koud [*kood*]	elbow
lou [*loo*]	heavy
mou [*moo*]	soft
moun [*moon*]	people
nou [*noo*]	we, us
ouvè [*oo-ve*]	to open
ouvri [*oo-vree*]	to open
pou [*poo*]	for
pou l [*pool*]	for him/her
sou [*sue*]	on, drunk, inebriated
tou [*too*]	too
tout [*toot*]	all
tous [*toos*]	cough
youn [*yoon*]	one

Sample Sentences – OU

Kreyòl	English
Mwen santi on doulè nan kou	I feel some pain in my neck
Met plat la sou tab la	Put the plate on the table
Mwen tou	Me too
M ap vini tou	I am coming too
Li ban M tout	She gave it all to me
Ti moun yo ap jwe boul	The kids are playing ball
Kochon yo ap jwe nan la bou a	The pigs are playing in the mud
Se pa kou M k ap fè M mal; se koud mwen	It's not my neck that's hurting; it's my elbow
Ou! bouyon an gou	Wow, the stew tastes good
Mwen pito soup jouwoumou	I prefer squash soup
Ki ès nan yo de a ki kouri pi dousman	Of the two of them, who 's the slowest runner
Ki ès nan yo de a ki pi dousman	Who's the most docile of the two

Konvèsasyon

The following is a konvèsasyon between a traveler and a customs agent who is checking the content of the traveler's suitcase.

Bonjou	Good Morning
Bonjou, mesye, konbyen malèt ou genyen?	Good morning, sir, how many suitcases do you have?
Mwen gen twa malèt	I have three
Tanpri mete yo sou tab la pou mwen	Please put them on the table
Tout? Ou vle pou M ouvè tout?	All of them? You want me to open all of them?
Wi, men pa an mèm tan; ouvè yo youn apre lòt (souri)	Yes, but not at the same time; open them one by one (smile)
Sa a tou?	This one too?
Wi, tout nèt, mesye	Yes, sir, all of them
M pa genyen anyen serye nan malèt yo non	I don't have anything important in the suitcases
M pa di otreman	I didn't say otherwise
Se rad sèlman ki nan malèt yo wi	I only have some clothes in the suitcases
En ben, nan ka sa a li pap pran anpil tan	Well, in that case it won't take long
(Apre de twa minit) Mèsi mesye; M espere W pase on bon moman	*(A few minutes later)* Thank you; enjoy your stay

52-   THE BLEND WA (WA)

Wa_[wah]

Wa is a substitute for *oi* or *oy*. It sounds just like **wa** in *water*. **Wa** is also a word that means *King*. There are certain cases where there's a space that separates *W*, the abbreviated form of the pronoun *ou* and the verb it modifies that begins with *a*. In those cases, the space doesn't affect the phonetics and the pronunciation is still *was* like in *water*. Here are a few egzanp:

W al or **W ale** means **you go**

W admire means **you admire**

W adore means **you adore**

W aprann means **you learn**

W aksepte means **you accept**

W apresye means **you apreciate**

W anonse means **you announce**

W antre means **you enter**

W antere means **you bury**

Common "Wa" Words

Kreyòl	English
bwa *[bwah]*	wood
bwate *[bwah-tey]*	to limp
bway *[bwahy]*	boy
chwa *[shwah]*	choice
dwa *[dwah]*	right
dwat *[dwaht]*	right, straight
espwa *[ehs-pwah]*	hope
eksplwa *[ehx-plwah]*	exploit
eksplwate *[ehx-plwah-tey]*	to exploit
fwa *[fwah]*	time, liver
jwa *[zhwah]*	joy
jwaye *[zhwah-ee-ey]*	joyful
kwa *[kwah]*	cross
lwa *[lwah]*	law
la lwa *[lah-lwah]*	aloe
mwa *[mwah]*	month
mwatye *[mwah-tee-ey]*	half
nwa *[nwah]*	black
pwa *[pwah]*	peas, weight
pwason *[pwah-sohN]*	fish
pwazon *[pwah-zohN]*	poison
swa *[swah]*	evening, smooth
vwa *[vwah]*	voice
vwayaj *[vwah-ee-ahzh]*	trip
vwazen *[vwah-zehN]*	neighbor *(male)*
vwazin *[vwah-zeen]*	neighbor *(female)*
wa *[wah]*	king, you will
twa *[twah]*	three
zwazo *[zwah-zoh]*	bird

Sample Sentences – WA

Kreyòl	English
Mwen pa gen chwa	I have no choice
Li santi L jwaye lè ti moun nan tounen lakay li	He felt so joyful when the kid came back home
Vwazen an byen netwaye machin nan	The neighbor did a good job cleaning the car
Lè N vwayaje, vwazin an voye jye sou kay la pou nou	When we travel, our neighbor keeps an eye on our house
Mwen renmen di ri a pwa	I like rice and beans
Ti bebe a an fòm; M wè li pran on ti pwa	The baby looks good; I see he gained some weight
M ap vwayaje nan twa mwa	I'm travelling in three months
Malad la gen on pwoblèm nan fwa	The patient has a problem in her liver
Li di L ap fè on mwa Ayiti	She said she'll spend one month in Haiti
Chantè a gen bèl vwa	The singer has a beautiful voice

Konvèsasyon

I hope you are heading to a Creole speaking country soon. When you do, you will inevitably have a konvèsasyon similar to the one below. If you check in any suitcases at an airport, there will be plenty of baggage handlers (BH) who will offer their assistance to locate them. I may have mentioned a few times already that Haitians are polite. They will start by greeting you. They will then offer to locate your luggage and bring it to you while you wait. The konvèsasyon will go something like this:

(I suggest you practice both roles to get a feel for the very useful words and expressions we use in dialogue).

BH: Bon swa, madam, kòman ou ye?	Good afternoon, ma'am, how are you?
You: Mwen byen, e ou menm?	I am well, how about you?
BH: Ou jwenn malèt ou deja?	Did you already find your suitcases?
You: Non, mwen poko	No, not yet
BH: Ban M al chache L pou ou	Let me go find it for you
You: OK	OK
BH: Konbyen malèt ou genyen?	Howmany suitcases do you have?
You: On sèl	Only one
BH: Ki koulè L?	What color is it?
You: Gri	Grey
BH: Ban M tikè a	Let me have the stub
You: Men ni	Here it is
BH: Men gen chèz la a wi, ou mèt chita	Here is a chair, please have a seat
BH: M ap vini a malèt la nan on lòt moman	I'll be back with the suitcase in a few minutes
You: Dakò, M ap ret tann ou	OK, I'll wait for you
BH: (Kèlke minit apre) Men ni wi, mwen jwenn ni	(A few minutes later) Here it is, I found it
You: Mèsi bokou	Thank you very much

53- THE BLEND WO (WO)

 **W**o *[woh]*

R in front of *o* like in *project,* is replaced with a *w*. With that in mind, let's take a look at one of the most interesting Kreyòl words, *womans.* This is not a poor English student's attempt at the plural form of *woman,* this is the correct spelling of a Kreyòl word that means *romance* or *romantic novel.*

An analysis of the word *womans* teaches you quite a bit about writing Kreyòl and enhances your ability to spot certain cognates that you come across. If the ending of a word would be *se* or *ce* in English or French, it's just *s* in Kreyòl. The *r* in *romance* is barely pronounced in Kreyòl. For that reason, it's substituted with *w*.

Common Words with Wo and Wò blends

Kreyòl	English
bwonch [*bwohnNsh*]	bronchitis
bwòs [*bwos*]	brush
kontwòl [*kohN-twol*]	control
kontwole [*kohN-two-ley*]	to control
kwonik [*kwoh-neek*]	chronic
patwon [*pah-twohN*]	patron/boss
patwonaj [*pah-twoh-nahzh*]	patronage
pwobab [*pwoh-bahb*]	probable
pwoblèm [*pwoh-blem*]	problem
pwofesè [*pwoh-fey-se*]	professor

pwofi [pwoh-fee]	profit
pwofite [pwo-fee-tey]	to profit
pwogrè [pwoh-gre]	progress
pwogrese [pwoh-grey-sey]	to progress
pwojè [pwoh-zhe]	project
pwoteje [pwoh-tey-zhey]	to protect
pwoteksyon [pwoh-tek-see-ohN]	protection
powvèb [pwoh-veb]	proverb
powvens [pwoh-vehNs]	province
twoke [twoh-key]	to exchange
twopik [twoh-peek]	tropic
wòl [wall]	role

Sample sentences with Wo and Wò blends

Kreyòl	English
Moun ki ekri liv sa a se on trè bon pwofesè	The person who wrote this book is a very good teacher
Li vann ni men li pa fè pyès pwofi	He sold it without a profit
M pa gen pwoblèm a sa	I have no problem with that
Ou bezwen paking, patwon?	Do you need a parking spot, boss?
M ap lave machin nan pou ou, patwon	I'll wash the car for you, boss
Li pa gen kontwòl sitiyasyon an	He isn't in control of the situation
Pot bwòs la ban M pou M penyen cheve W	Bring me the brush so I can comb your hair
Ou pa bezwen gen pwoblèm, mwen la pou M pwoteje W	No need to worry, I am here to protect you
Djòb mwen se ba W pwoteksyon	My job is to protect you

In closing, the following is some late additions to your vocabulary:

Popular Verbs / Vèb Popilè			
renmen	to love, like	damou	to fall in love
rayi	to hate	deteste	to detest
priye	to pray	kriye	to cry
mennen	to lead, take somewhere	trennen	to drag
deplase	to move	siveye	to watch
pwoteje	to protect	konte	to count
kontwole	to control	etidye	to study
repare	to repair	pentire	to paint
netwaye	to clean	siye	to wipe
anonse	to announce	koupe	to cut
konpoze	to compose	kraze	to break
vizite	to visit	kondi	to drive
achte	to buy	vann	to sell
machande	to bargain	kuit	to cook
kanpe	to stand up	mache	to walk
chita	to sit down	kouche	to lay down
kouri	to run	dòmi	to sleep
mouri	to die	resisite	to resuscitate
ranje	to fix	reziste	to resist

The typical translation for the preposition *at* like in *"at the airport"* is **nan**, but it's sometimes omitted in expressions like **kay doktè a**, **kay dantis la** meaning *at the doctor's* and *at the dentist* respectively.

Places / Kèk Kote			
nan dispansè a	at the klinik	lòt bò	foreign country
nan mòg la	at the morgue	nan simityè a	at the cemetery
nan ayewopò a, èpòt	airport	kwen	corner
nan dlo	at the river	nan la rivyè a	at the river
nan lan mè	at the beach	sou plaj la	at the beach

nan bal la	at the ball	nan fèt la	at the party
nan match la	at the game	nan estad la	at the stadium
nan kabann nan	in bed	sou chèz la	on the chair
nan la ri a	on the street	nan chemen an	on the road

Now that you've reached the end of this book, I hope you feel more comfortable speaking, reading, and hearing Kreyòl. Use the tools I've given you (Relate2Remember, cognates, substitution rules, the similarity to English, etc) to continue in your Kreyòl-learning journey. Take advantage of the free YouTube videos available on my channel or on my website at wwww.haiti2030.org to practice your pronunciation. When you go on your next trip to Haiti, you'll be ready!

Onè and *respè*!

Jacques Julmice

Appendix A

General Every Day Expressions

English	Kreyòl
Hello	Alo or Bonjou
Goodbye	Babay or M ale
Good evening	Bon swa or bòn sware
Good night	Bòn nui or Bòn nuit
See you later	Na wè
See you another time	Ma wè W on lòt lè
Thank you	Mèsi
Thank you very much	Mèsi bokou or mèsi anpil
Please	Tanpri or souple or sil vou plè
Pretty please	Tanpri souple
Please explain	Tanpri eksplike
Please repeat	Tanpri repete
Repeat slowly	Repete dousman
Please tell me	Tanpri di M
Please give me	Tanpri ban M
You're welcome	Pa gen pwoblèm
No problem	Pa gen danje (modern)
Excuse me	Ekskize M
Do you know?	Èske W konn or konnen?
Do you have?	Èske W gen or genyen?
Can you help me?	Ou ka ede M?
Can you show me?	Ou ka montre M?
How?	Kòman or kouman or ki jan?
How do you say ?	Kòman ou di or kòman W di?
How do you pronounce?	Kouman W pwononse?
Pronounce it slowly	Pwononse L dousman
What does that mean?	Kisa sa vle di?
What do you mean?	Kisa W vle di?
I need	Mwen bezwen

I want	Mwen vle
I would like	Mwen ta renmen
What did you say?	Kisa W di? or kisa ou di?
I'm lost	Mwen pèdi
I'm looking for	M ap chache or M ap chèche
Do you speak English?	Ès ke ou pale Anglè?
Do you understand English?	Ès ke ou konprann Anglè?
I understand	Mwen konprann
I understand very little Creole	Mwen konprann Kreyòl tou piti
I don't understand	Mwen pa konprann
I understand all that you say	Mwen konprann tout sa W di
I barely understand	Mwen prèske pa konprann anyen
I remember	Mwen sonje
I don't remember anything	Mwen pa sonje anyen
I need a taxi	Mwen bezwen on taksi
Please call me a taxi	Tanpri rele on taksi pou mwen
I'm waiting for a cab	M ap ret tann taksi
What's your name?	Ki non W? or Ki jan ou rele?
My name is …	Mwen rele …
How old are you?	Ki laj ou?
I arrived last week	Mwen rive semèn pase
I'm leaving next Saturday	M ap pati lòt Samdi

At the Restaurant or Bar

English	Kreyòl
I'm hungry	Mwen grangou
I'm full	Vant mwen plen
I'm thirsty	Mwen swaf
I'd like a cold beer	M ta bwè on byè byen frape
Where is a restaurant?	Ki bò ki gen on restoran?
Is the food ready?	Ès ke manje a pare?
It isn't ready yet	Li poko pare
The food is almost ready	Manje a prèske pare
When will it be ready?	A ki lè L ap pare?
Do you want to taste?	Ou vle goute?
Don't put any sugar in the juice	Pa mete sik nan ji a
I don't want a lot of sugar	Mwen pa vle anpil sik
Very little sugar	On ti sik tou piti
May I have some water?	Ou ka ban Mon ti dlo?
A glass of wine please	On vè di ven sil vou plè
I like red wine	Mwen renmen di ven wouj
I prefer white wine	Mwen pito di ven blan
I would like some juice	M ta renmen en pe ji
I'll have a coke	M ap pran on koka
Give me a cola please	Ban M on kola sil vou plè
I am alone	Mwen pou kont mwen
Only me	Mwen sèlman
I don't want a lot of food	M pa vle anpil manje
That's enough	Sa a kont or sa a sifi or sa a ase
I want more	M vle ankò
Put some more	Mete toujou
The food is spicy	Manje a pike
Don't put hot pepper for me	Pa met piman pou mwen
Bring it to my room	Pote L nan chanm mwen an
How do you want your eggs?	Ki jan ou vle ze yo?

I don't like my eggs well done	M pa renmen ze ki kwit anpil
I don't like onions	Mwen pa renmen zonyon
M fè alèji a zonyon	I'm allergic to onions
Be careful, it's hot	Fè atansyon, li cho
I really like this	M renmen sa a anpil
This is really good	Li bon anpil papa
How do you call it?	Kòman ou rele L?
How do you call this thing?	Ki jan ou rele bagay sa a?
How do you say it?	Ki jan ou di L?
Please remove it	Tanpri retire L
Did I say it right?	Ès ke mwen di L byen?
Is there anymore?	Ès ke genyen ankò?
May I have some more?	Ou ka ban M en pe ankò?
You may put some more	Ou mèt mete toujou
I'll tell you when to stop	M ap di W ki lè pou ou rete
You may pour some more	Ou mèt vide toujou
Give me some	Ban M en pe
Give me some more	Ban M on ti kras an plis
Give me just a little	Ban M on ti kras tou piti
The bread isn't fresh	Pen an pa fre
The beer isn't cold	Byè a pa byen glase
The mango is rotten	Mango a pouri
The apple isn't ripe	Pòm nan pa mi
The wine doesn't tate good	Di ven an pa gen bon gou
The milk is expired	Lèt la ekspire
The meat is salty	Vyann nan sale

At the Bank

English	Kreyòl
Where is the bank?	Kote bank la ye?
Can you take me to the bank?	Ou ka mennen M nan bank la?
I need to exchange my money	M bezwen chanje lajan
What is the exchange rate?	Konbyen lajan ameriken an ye?
What are the banking hours?	A ki lè bank la ouvè?
What time does the bank close?	A ki lè bank la fèmen?
The bank is secure	Gen sekirite nan bank la
I have an account at the bank	Mwen gen on kont nan bank la
I'd like to open an account	Mwen ta renmen ouvè on kont
I don't have my bank card	M pa gen kat bank mwen an
Yes I remember my PIN	Wi, Mwen sonje nimewo kòd la
Do I have to show you my ID?	Fò M montre W kat idantite M?
Can you help me?	Ou ka ede M?
Who is the boss in the office?	Ki ès ki patwon an nan biwo a?
Can I see the director?	M ka wè direktè a?
I'd like to speak to a supervisor	M ta renmen pale a on sipèvizè
Has the director arrived yet?	Ès ke direktè a rive deja?
Who can provide that info?	Ki ès ki ban M enfòmayon sa a?
Is there anyone else who can help?	Ès ke on lòt moun ki da ede M?

At the Hotel

English	Kreyòl
I'm staying five nights	M ap fè senk jou
My reservation is for only one night	M gen rezèvasyon pou on sèl nuit
What's the nightly rate?	Ki pri chanm nan pa nuit?
What's my room number?	Ki nimewo chanm mwen an?
What floor is the room on?	Nan ki etaj chanm nan ye?
I prefer a king size bed	M pito on sèl gwo kabann
Do you have WiFi?	Èske gen Wifi?
Is breakfast included?	Èske peti dejene a gratis?
I only need one key	Ou mèt ban M on sèl kle
I traveled alone	Mwen vwayaje pou kont mwen
My family is flying in tomorrow	Fanmi M ap vini demen
I've stayed at the hotel before	Mwen te rete nan otèl la deja
I know my way around	Mwen konn kote pou M ale
That's my first time at the hotel	Se premye fwa M ret nan otèl la
I don't like this room	Mwen pa renmen chanm sa a
I'd like a different room	M vle on lòt chanm
The AC is broken	È kondisyone a an pàn
The Wifi doesn't work	Wifi la pa mache
Yes, the Wifi works	Wi, Wifi la mache

At the Hospital

English	Kreyòl
I came to visit my friend	Mwen vin wè on zanmi M
Where's the patient?	Kot malad la?
What do you feel?	Kisa W santi?
He's gotten better	Li miyò
She isn't feeling well	Li pa santi L byen
They gained weight	Yo pran pwa
They lost too much weight	Yo pèdi twòp pwa
She feels great now	Li santi L an fòm kounyè a
Surgey isn't necessary	Nou pap bezwen fè operasyon
How long have you felt like this?	Depi ki lè ou santi W konsa?
Have you taken your medication?	Ès ke ou pran medikaman W?
Does that hurt?	Ès ke sa a fè mal?
Tell me if it hurts	Di M si L fè W mal
Do you feel any pain?	Ès ke ou santi doulè?
Breathe	Respire
Hold your breath	Kenbe souf ou
Breathe normally	Respire nòmal
It won't hurt	Li pap fè W mal
It won't hurt at all	Li pap fè mal pyès
You won't feel any more pain	Ou pap santi doulè ankò
You made a lot of progress	Ou fè anpil pwogrè
You're six weeks pregnant	Ou gen sis semèn ansent
You'll have the baby in May	W ap akouche an Me
It's a boy	Se on ti gason
Did you prefer a girl?	Ou te pito on ti fi?
You're going to have twins	W ap fè marasa
Are you happy?	Ou kontan?
How is the baby?	Kòman ti bebe a ye?
The baby is healthy	Bebe a an sante
Both mom and baby are well	Ni manman ni bebe a an fòm

Religious

English	Kreyòl
Pray for them	Priye pou yo
I'll pray for you	M ap priye pou ou
Where is the pastor?	Kot pastè a?
I'm reading my bible	M ap li bib mwen
Do you believe in Jesus?	Ès ke ou kwè nan Jezi?
What's your favorite verse?	Ki vèsè ou pi renmen?
Personally I love Psaume 23	Mwen renmen Sòm 23
What book do you prefer?	Ki liv ou pi renmen?
I prefer the book of Paul	M pi renmen liv Paul la
Tell me a bible story	Rakonte M on istwa nan bib la
I'm going to church with you	Mwen pwal legliz avè W
Can I invite you to church?	M ka envite W al legliz?
Are you baptized?	Ès ke ou batize?
Are you saved?	Ès ke ou sove?
Where do you go to church?	Ki kote W al legliz?
What religion do you follow?	Ki relijyon W?
I'm catholic	Mwen se katolik
I'm a protestant	M se pwotestan
Do you accept Jesus as your savior?	Ès ke W aksepte Jezi kòm sovè W?

Appendix B

VOCABULARY

Same spelling and Meaning

English	Kreyòl
to admire	admire
to adore	adore
to agonize	agonize
anti	anti
Arab	Arab
bank	bank
baton	baton
bravo	bravo
demon	demon
divan	divan
to double, to pass	double
final	final
gratis	gratis
idol	idòl
to lave, to wash	lave
legal	legal
liberal	liberal
limit	limit
long	long
mango	mango
mason	mason
match	match
to memorize	memorize
merit	merit

metal	metal
moral	moral
napkin	napkin
to note	note
patch	patch
pin	pin
piston	piston
plan	plan
planet	planèt
plant	plant
to prepare	prepare
rat	rat
to revoke, to fire	revoke
salad	salad
siren	sirèn
solid	solid
soup	soup
switch	switch
tank	tank
timid	timid
total	total
to vote	vote
veteran	veteran
vital	vital
vitamin	vitamin
zip	zıp

Appendix C

COMMON VOCABULARY

English	Kreyòl
acts	zak
all	tout
to allot	lote
arm	bra
army	lame
to arrive	rive
ashamed	wont
aspirin	aspirin
august	out
autobus	bis
back	do
bad, frown	move
to be ready	pare
to beat up	bat
to beat up, to peal	kale
belly	pans
bench, to give	ban
between	ant
to block	bare
to bounce (ball)	mate
bread	pen
broke (no money)	razè
broom, to sweep	bale
to carry	pot
to cite	site
crowd	foul

didn't	pa t
dirty	sal
dirty	sire
discolored	fane
door	pòt
drama	dram
dress	rad
drop	gout
to empty	vide
to engrave, to inscribe	grave
faded	blaze
to fart	pete
to finish	fin (short for fini)
foam	kim
frank	fran
garlic	lay
gift (divine, charity)	don
to give	bay
global	global
to go	al (short for ale)
to go	ale
gossip	zen
grade	grad
grave, accent on e or o	grav
hand	men
hat	bone
hat	bonè
he or she is + ing	l ap
head start (before running)	elan
his, hers pronou	pa l
honor	onè
house, home	kay

to hunt	chase
hunter	chasè
to be + ing	ap
to inhale	aspire
to lace	lase
to last	dire
later	talè
to leave, let	kite
to lick	niche
living room	salon
to look, policeman	gad
manner	jan
to mark	make
to master	doze
may	me
mentally challenged	vivi
mine pronoun	pa m
motivated	motive
motorcycle	moto
notary public	notè
notebook, curdling	kaye
old, big	gran
one	on
ours pronoun	pa n
oval	oval
owner, must, meter	mèt
painting	pent
palace	palè
to pass	pase
plate	plat
to poke, to stab, spicy, hot	pike
to pound	plane

to put	met
pastry	pate
peacock	pan
photo	foto
please	souple
rank	grade
to remark	remake
rest	repo
to remove	retire
request	demand
ring	bag
roman	women
romantic novel	woman
round	won
row	ran
saint (feminine)	sent
salty	sale
to scratch	grate
serenade	serenad
to shave	raze
to shoot (gun)	tire
slap	tap
to slap	tape
so much	pit
sound	son
sound	ton
to speak	pale
spoiled, rotten, bad	gate
to spread out	gaye
stable	stab
to step on	pile
straw mat	nat

straw, dust	pay
to stumble	bite
supper	dine
to swallow	vale
to sweat	transpire
table	tab
table cloth	nap
tasteless	fad
the year	lane
thin, sharp (well dressed)	fen
thin, slim	mens
thursday	jedi
time, weather	tan
to thread	file
to tie down	mare
too	twò
tooth	dan
tripe, intestines	trip
type	tip
ugly	lèd
value	valè
vote	vòt
to walk, market	mache
we are + ing	n ap
to wear (casual clothings)	drive
whether	kit
wind	van
romance	womans
word	mo
would	t ap
yours	pa w
to zip	zipe

Appendix D

Single Letter Words

Words	Pronunciation	English
a	a *[ah]*	the
e	e *[ey]*	and, how about
è	e *[e]*	air
k	ki *[kee]*	who, that
L	li *[lee]*	he/she/it
M	mwen *[mwehn]*	I
N	nou *[noo]*	we
N	nou *[noo]*	you (plural)
o	o *[oh]*	oh
t	te *[tey]*	past tense
W	ou *[oo]*	you (singular)
Y	yo *[yoh]*	they

Appendix E

Two-Letter Words

Kreyòl	English
ak	with
al (abbreviation for ale)	to go
an	the
ap	progressive form (ing)
ba	low
bè	butter
bi	goal
bo	kiss, to kiss, handsome
bò	side
de	two
dè	many
di	hard
do	back
èd	aid
èn	hatred
ès	is, east
fa	lipstick
fè	to do, iron
fe (di fe)	fire
fi	girl
fo	fake
fò	strong
ge	joy, merriment
gè	war
il	island
im	hymn
in	one
ja	treasure
je	eye, play
jè	spray, fountain (water)

ji	juice
ka	can, case
ke	that
kè	heart
ki	who
kò	body, callus
la	the, there
le	the
lè	time, when
li	he, she, it
lo	lot, prize
lò	gold
ma	I, residue
mè	old lady, sea
mi	ripe, wall
mo	word
mò	dead person
na	we
ne	node
nè	nerves
ni	either, he, she, it
nò	north
òd	order
òf	offer
on	a, one
ou	you, or
pa	not, step
pe	to be quiet
pè	father, old man, peace, pair
pi	more
po	skin
pò	port, pores
ra	rare
ri	street, to laugh

sa	that
se	it's
sè	sister
si	if, sure
so, syo	seal, bucket (of water)
sò	girlfriend
ta	would, late
te	past tense mark, tea
tè	earth, dirt
ti	small
to	rate
tò	at fault
va	to go, will
ve	wish
vè	worm
vi	life
vo	value
wa	king
wè	to see
wi	yes
wo	high, tall
ye	to be
ya	they
yo	they
ze	egg
zè	time, hour
zo	bond

Appendix F

COMMON PHRASES

Kreyòl	English
Ki non W?	What's your name?
Non M se Jacky	My name is Jacky
Ki jan ou rele?	What do they call you?
Mwen rele Nancy	They call me Nancy
Ki jan ou ye?	How are you?
Mwen byen	I'm well
Ki jan ou santi W?	How do you feel?
Mwen santi M byen	I feel good
Mèsi	Thank you
De ryen	You're welcome
Pa gen pwoblèm	No problem
Padon / Ekskize M	Pardon / Excuse me
M ta renmen	I would like
Mwen bezwen	I need
Mwen konprann	I understand
M pa konprann	I don't understand
Padone M	Forgive me
Ou ka ede M?	Can you help me?
Ès ke ou genyen?	Do you have?
Mwen pèdi	I'm lost
Kisa W vle di?	What do you mean
Ès ke ou vle?	Do you want?
Ès ke ou ka ban M?	Can you give me?
Ès ke ou ka di M?	Can you tell me?
Ès ke ou ka fè	Can you do?
M ap tann	I'll wait
M ap tann ou	I'm waiting for you
N ap chache	We're looking for

Made in the USA
Middletown, DE
17 September 2020